WOLVES
Miscellany

WOLVES
Miscellany

Wanderers Trivia,
History, Facts & Stats

JOHN HENDLEY

THE WOLVES MISCELLANY

WANDERERS HISTORY, TRIVIA, FACTS & STATS

All statistics, facts and figures are correct as of 1st August 2007

© John Hendley

John Hendley has asserted his rights in accordance with the Copyright, Designs and Patents Act 1988 to be identified as the author of this work.

Published By:
Pitch Publishing (Brighton) Ltd
A2 Yeoman Gate
Yeoman Way
Durrington
BN13 3QZ

Email: info@pitchpublishing.co.uk
Web: www.pitchpublishing.co.uk

First published 2007

A catalogue record for this book is available from the British Library.

10-digit ISBN: 1-9054110-6-5
13-digit ISBN: 978-1-9054110-6-1

Printed and bound in India by Replika Press Pvt. Ltd.

FOREWORD BY STEVE BULL MBE

A few days after I arrived at Wolves, in November, 1986, I began to wonder exactly what I had done. I watched from the stands as the team lost to non-League Chorley in the FA Cup. The club was also struggling in the wrong half of the Fourth Division table.

But, even in those bleak times, I was aware of the sleeping giant that was waiting for a wake-up call. I also quickly realised how desperate the supporters were to see the name of Wolverhampton Wanderers back challenging for top honours.

Although originally a Liverpool fan, Molineux soon became my footballing home and I began to learn of the tradition of this magnificent club. I met football legends such as Billy Wright and Ron Flowers, Bert Williams and Peter Broadbent – some of the game's all-time greats.

And, of course, there are the supporters. Men, women, boys and girls who would spend their last few quid on following the club that they were so passionate about. I spent virtually the whole of my career at Wolves and consider myself very fortunate to have done so.

Much has been written about the club but this new book has a different slant to it. All the great days are recalled along with facts, figures and trivia - some of which is quirky to say the least.

The book has been well compiled by John Hendley, or 'Fozzie' as everyone at the club knows him, and I would like to wish him every success with this Wolves Miscellany.

Steve Bull MBE
Wolverhampton Wanderers FC 1986 – 1999

INTRODUCTION

Who were all these people making their way past our house in Red Lion Street? Where were they going and why did they look so happy and excited? When, as a five-year-old, I put the question to my mother, she replied that "They are going to the match".

It was only as the years rolled by, and after we had moved to another part of town, I realised that our old house was little more than a corner-kick away from Molineux at a time when Wolves were enjoying their finest hours.

The fifties proved to be Wolves' zenith but there had already been some memorable achievements since the club came into life as St Lukes in 1877. Wolves were founder members of the Football League, the FA Cup was won against all the odds in 1908, and some truly great players had donned the famous old gold and black.

My first flirtation with football came when I went along to watch Wolves and Charlton Athletic play a Second Division fixture at Molineux in November, 1965. As I made my way into the old South Bank for the first time, I was hit by a barrage of noise and colour that made an instant impression. The excitement grew as the teams took to the field and it rose to a crescendo when Hughie McIlmoyle found the net. It was the first goal I had seen and I looked around in awe as people, male and female, young and old, celebrated as if they had just been given the formula for an everlasting life.

However, for every football fan, there will also be bad days and Wolves supporters have had their share of those over the years. But the passion has always remained along with the desire to see Wanderers in the headlines for all the right reasons.

Now, on a matchday, as I watch these thousands of people making their way to the ground, I know where they are going – and I know why they are looking so expectant.

For me, if I'm not watching football then I love to be talking about it - especially to the players and supporters of years gone by. People who played a part in the club's history or watched as events unfolded before them.

I hope that this book will bring back some happy memories and it will offer some snippets of information to even the most learned of supporters.

John Hendley

GENESIS

The Blakenhall area of Wolverhampton was the birthplace of the team that we now know as Wolverhampton Wanderers. It was in Lower Villiers Street that St. Luke's School, adjacent to the church, saw the beginnings of the club when Harry Barcroft, the school's young headmaster, is reputed to have presented a football to two of his scholars after they had enjoyed a successful academic year. Those scholars, Jack Brodie and Jack Baynton, soon involved fellow pupils in their plans to form a team and the first general meeting of the Goldthorn Football Club was called on Friday November 10, 1876. The poster advertising the meeting requested 'Any Gentleman interested in playing the game is invited to attend'. Less than 10 weeks later the first recorded game of what had become known as Blakenhall St. Luke's took place against the team from the town's railway works, Stafford Road, who, despite fielding a reserve team, were comfortable 8-0 victors. In 1879, St. Luke's merged with the nearby Blakenhall Cricket and Football Club to become Wolverhampton Wanderers. In the four years since formation, the team played at the Windmill Field and John Harpers Field – both of which were within easy reach of St. Luke's. Then, in 1881, the club switched to a new ground on Dudley Road opposite the Fighting Cocks pub. It offered little by way of protection from the elements with a small lean-to the only cover. In 1883, the club participated in the FA Cup for the first time before, five years later, they became founder members of the Football League. The move to Molineux came the following summer shortly before the start of the second League season.

A DIFFERENT KIND OF HAT-TRICK

Having won 3-1 in The Hague against AZ Den Haag in a second round UEFA Cup match in 1971, Wolves were expected to progress to the next stage of the competition. But they got a surprise helping hand from their Dutch opponents in the second leg at Molineux with three defenders – Kees Weiner, Aad Mansveld and Theo Van Den Burch – all putting through their own goal. Derek Dougan was the solitary scorer from the home team that night as Wolves progressed to meet Carl Ziess Jena with a 7-1 aggregate.

DOUBLE UPS FOR CRAIG AND ROHAN

When Wolves travelled to Norwich in January, 2007, Craig Fleming achieved a rare double when he was named on the team page of the programme for both sides. The defender, who had been with the Canaries for 10 years, was spending a month with Wolves on an emergency loan. Ironically, he wasn't eligible to play for either team on the night of the game as he was still on loan and there was an agreement between the clubs that he wouldn't play against City during his short-term stay with Wolves. The day after the game he moved to Rotherham on a free transfer. Less than three months later, in similar circumstances, Rohan Ricketts featured in both team line-ups in the Wolves v Queens Park Rangers programme. The same agreement had been reached between the clubs with Ricketts unable to appear for either team. He was on loan at Loftus Road from Molineux at the time.

KNOCKOUT

Henry Cooper defended his Commonwealth and British Heavyweight Championships against Swadlincote chicken farmer Jack Bodell in a ring erected on the pitch at Molineux in June 1967. Bodell caused the Champion a few problems in the opening round but Cooper came out for the second with 'all guns blazing' to bludgeon Bodell into submission – the referee stopping the fight.

DOUBLE SIX

The scores from a pair of back-to-back games in Wolves' Second Division season of 1976/77 wouldn't have been out of place in a tennis match. On Saturday October 2, 1976, they played their first competitive match at Hereford's Edgar Street and goals from Willie Carr, Steve Daley, Steve Kindon and Alan Sunderland – along with a brace from Bobby Gould – saw Wanderers emerge as 6-1 victors. The following Tuesday, Daley and Kenny Hibbitt were on target when Southampton visited Molineux but this time it was Wolves' turn to be hit for six with the Saints travelling back to the south coast after a 6-2 win.

FA CUP FINAL 1889

In the first season of the Football League of 1888/89, Wolves, for the first time, made it through to the FA Cup Final which was played at Kennington Oval. In opposition was a Preston North End team that had taken the League title without losing a match and by dropping just four points out of a possible 44. Wolves had finished third in the table but they were no match for the Lancashire side whose exploits had earned them the name of The Invincibles. Tommy Knight did hit the post before Fred Dewhurst fired Preston into the lead and, by the interval, Jimmy Ross had made the score 2-0. Sammy Thomson completed the scoring 20 minutes before the end in front of a crowd of 22,500. Wolves' route to the final was as follows:

Round/scorers	Opponents/venue	Score
Round 1	Old Carthusians (h)	4-3
Mason, Wykes, Wood 2		
Round 2	Walsall Town Swifts (h)	6-1
Lowder, Hunt, Brodie, Knight 3		
Round 3	Sheffield Wednesday (h)	3-0
Fletcher, Wykes 2		
Semi-final	Blackburn Rovers (at Crewe)	1-1
Wykes		
SF replay	Blackburn Rovers (at Crewe)	3-1
Allen, Hunter, Wood		
Final	Preston North End (at Kennington Oval)	0-3

Wolves 1889 FA Cup Final team: Baynton, Baugh, Mason, Fletcher, Allen, Lowder, Hunter, Wykes, Brodie, Wood, Knight.

HEADS UP BOBBY

Bobby Woodruff scored all of Wolves' goals in 3-0 victory over Sunderland at Molineux on Easter Tuesday 1965. Nothing unusual in that perhaps, except that all three goals were headed. A crowd of under 15,000 watched the game with Wolves heading towards relegation.

LIVELY OPENING

Headed goals from Peter Broadbent and Jimmy Murray put Wolves two up after just two minutes in a First Division Molineux meeting with Newcastle United in October 1959. But if the home supporters in the near-34,000 crowd were expecting a goal bonanza they were to be disappointed, for the 88 minutes that followed yielded no further score.

JUST MISSED OUT

Wolves' first season in the Fourth Division, 1987/88, ended in agonising fashion. Seemingly out of contention for promotion at the end of January, the side put together a magnificent run that saw them winning 15 times and picking up 47 points from the 57 available from the final 19 games of the campaign. Any other season in the Fourth Division would have resulted in automatic promotion for the fourth-placed team – the berth occupied by Wolves who finished a point behind Southend United who were third. Wolves had the better goal difference so one more point would have seen them promoted. But 1988 marked the first year of the play-offs and, after beating Colchester United on aggregate in the semi-finals, Wolves lost 3-0 over the two legs of the final against an Aldershot team they had done the double over in League fixtures during the season.

DAMAGE LIMITATION

Portsmouth manager George Smith will doubtless have had little more than damage limitation on his mind when his players returned to the visitors' dressing room at Molineux at half-time during a Second Division fixture in November 1965. A rampant Wolves side had raced into a 6-0 lead by the break with Bobby Woodruff, who hit two, Dave Wagstaffe, Hugh McIlmoyle, Ron Flowers and John Holsgrove all finding the back of the net. Pompey's defence tightened up significantly in a second half played in a snowstorm with the teams sharing four goals – making the final score 8-2 to Wanderers.

JIMMY MURRAY: EARLY GOAL AGAINST NEWCASTLE

LEAGUE CUP FIRST

Wolves didn't enter the League Cup until the seventh year of its existence. Mansfield Town were their first opponents in a second round tie at Molineux in September 1966 and Bob Hatton, making his debut, scored the winning goal in the 53rd minute to complete the come-back after the Third Division team had taken a 15th minute lead through Bill Curry. The honour of being the first League Cup goalscorer for Wolves fell to Terry Wharton who cracked a 36th-minute equaliser. A crowd of just 13,098 watched the 2-1 win. Hatton also scored after just 30 seconds of his League debut against Portsmouth 25 days later. He was to hit eight goals in 13 games in a brief Molineux career before he was transferred to Bolton towards the end of that 1966/67 campaign.

LATE REVIVAL

Sheffield United substitute Nathan Blake, later to play for Wolves, must have thought that he had earned his side the three points in January 1995 when he netted twice because, for all their efforts, the home players could find no way past United keeper Alan Kelly in the 90 minutes. Many of the near-28,000 crowd had left the ground when, on the stroke of full-time, Don Goodman latched onto a sloppy back pass and was felled in the area by Kelly. John de Wolf converted the spot kick and, with 92 minutes 17 seconds on the clock, Robbie Dennison centred for Neil Emblen to send a looping header into the net, earning Wolves a point that had looked lost.

LONGEST NAME

Wolves have got the longest name in any of the four senior English leagues. The full name of Wolverhampton Wanderers contains 22 letters, just one more than 'runners-up' Brighton and Hove Albion. Wolves took over the record when Scunthorpe and Lindsey United dropped the 'and Lindsey' from their name. But, if Scotland is included in the equation, then Inverness Caledonian Thistle would push Wolves down into second spot.

LATE GOAL RUSH

Any early leavers from Wolves' First Division clash with Chelsea at Molineux in September 1951 will have been left wondering what exactly had gone on following their departure. With five minutes of the game remaining Wolves were coasting at 4-0 before a late four-goal spurt saw a final outcome of 5-3 in favour of Stan Cullis' side.

TWO LEGS

There has only been one season when FA Cup ties in England were decided over two legs. It came in 1945/46 as the competition resumed after the war years and Wolves were drawn against non-League opposition in the third round in the shape of Lovells Athletic – the works team of the sweet manufacturers based at Newport in South Wales. Wolves had a bit of a shock in store in the first leg at Rexville going two goals down before hitting back to win 4-2. The return was a much more clear-cut affair with Wolves netting eight times and Lovells responding just once. Amongst the scorers for Wanderers were Tom Galley with a hat-trick and Billy Wright with two. Charlton Athletic provided the opposition in the next round and, after a 5-2 beating at the Valley, Wolves exited the competition after managing just a one-all draw in the second leg against that year's eventual losing finalists.

LAST AMATEUR

In 1951 Bill Slater became the last amateur to play in an FA Cup Final when he turned out for Blackpool against Newcastle United. The Tangerines lost 2-0 and later that year he joined Brentford before, in August 1952, he signed for Wolves. Two years later he signed semi-professional terms with the club – a status he maintained until retirement, resisting the temptation to turn fully pro'. After tasting the bitter pill of defeat against the Geordies, there was a much happier day for Bill in May 1960 when he led Wolves to FA Cup glory against Blackburn Rovers. His medal went nicely with the three he won when Wanderers captured the League Championship in the fifties.

FOUNDER MEMBERS

Wolverhampton Wanderers are one of the 12 founder members of the Football League which held its inaugural season in 1888/89. The teams, which were all from either the Midlands or the north-west of England, were: Accrington FC, Aston Villa, Blackburn Rovers, Bolton Wanderers, Burnley, Derby County, Everton, Notts County, Preston North End, Stoke City, West Bromwich Albion and Wolves. Playing in what was their final season at the Dudley Road ground, Wolves had four home fixtures to begin with, starting with a derby against Aston Villa. The game finished in a one-all draw with Villa coming back from a goal down after their full-back, Gershom Cox, had put through his own goal to gift Wanderers their historic first League goal. The first away match was at Accrington when the teams fought out a 4-4 draw. Wolves finished the season in a respectable third place – a point behind Villa – but 11 behind runaway champions Preston.

WIPED OUT BY WAR

The three games played by Wolves at the start of the 1939/40 season were expunged from the records as the world was plunged into war. The three lost games were:

Arsenal (home) 2-2
Grimsby Town (away) 0-0
Blackpool (away) 1-2

GOAL FEASTS

Despite scoring, Bobby Woodruff found himself out of favour following Southampton's 9-3 trouncing of Wolves at The Dell in September 1965. In the 10 weeks that followed the defeat, Wolves were unbeaten with five wins and four draws. Then came the home fixture with Portsmouth, Saints' bitter south coast rivals, when Woodruff was reinstated in the team. This time he bagged two as Wolves ran out 8-2 winners. In what were for the inside forward consecutive games, albeit 70 days apart, 22 goals were scored.

FA CUP FINAL 1893

Four of the players that had featured in Wolves' first FA Cup Final appearance against Preston four years previously – Dickie Baugh, Harry Allen, David Wykes and Harry Wood – had a much more lucrative afternoon when Wanderers made it through to a second final, against Everton, in March 1893. The final was played for the first and only time at Fallowfield, in Manchester, at the home of the Manchester Athletic Club. The 45,000 crowd that turned up for the game was far too large for the venue and the police on duty had their work cut out to clear the touchlines after spectators had encroached onto the playing area before kick-off. At one stage, with the police struggling to maintain order, the game looked to be in doubt. Everton were favourites to take the Cup back to Merseyside but the only goal, which came on the hour mark, came from Wolves skipper Harry Allen who beat the Everton keeper Richard Williams with a long-range effort. Williams appeared to have the shot covered but, depending on which report of the game you read, he either 'lost' the ball in the sun or was distracted by the crowd behind him. Wolves' route to the final was as follows:

Round/scorers	*Opponents/venue*	*Score*
Round 1	Bolton Wanderers (a)	1-1
Johnston		
Replay	Bolton Wanderers (h)	2-1
Wykes, Wood		
Round 2	Middlesbrough (h)	2-1
Wykes, Butcher		
Round 3	Darwin (h)	5-0
Topham 2, Wykes, Butcher, Griffin		
Semi-final	Blackburn Rovers (Town Ground, Notts)	2-1
Topham, Butcher		
Final	Everton (Fallowfield, Manchester)	1-0
Allen		

Wolves 1893 FA Cup Final team: Rose, Baugh, Swift, Malpass, Allen, Kinsey, Topham, Wykes, Butcher, Wood, Griffin.

FATHER AND SON IN THE MIDDLE

When Wolves met Coventry City at The Ricoh Arena in February 2009, they lost out to the Sky Blues by 2-1. The referee that afternoon was Michael Oliver. Seven days later the Molineux team suffered another defeat – this time by 1-0 to Burnley at Turf Moor. The man in the middle this time was Clive Oliver – the father of Michael.

SCHOOLBOY INTERNATIONAL WITH A DIFFERENCE

Academy scholar Johnny Gorman was still attending Repton School in Derbyshire when he won his first senior cap for Northern Ireland. The 17-year-old had played just Academy games and 30 minutes at reserve level for Wolves when he played for his country against Turkey in Connecticut in May, 2010. Sheffield born, he qualified as his mother Su originated from Northern Ireland. Studying A levels in Physical Education, English Literature and Art, Johnny divides his week between training with the Academy and his schoolwork.

WOLVES WIN THE ASHES

In the summer of 2009, Wolves embarked on a two week pre-season tour of Australia. Based in Perth the squad trained at The WACA – the world famous cricket test venue. WACA Communications co-ordinator Danny Davini came up with the idea of a mini test between the footballers and Western Australia's Retravision Warriors who were in the middle of their off season. Stephen Ward, Andy Surman, Sam Vokes, George Friend, Dave Edwards and Richard Stearman (three Englishmen, two Welsh and one Irish) represented England in the six a side, six overs a side, game whilst the Aussies included Brett Dorey, Luke Ronchi and Luke Pomersbach who had all played limited overs cricket for Australia. Aided and abetted by some more than generous amendments to the rules and some very questionable umpiring decisions, the footballers somehow made the 53 they needed to win with four balls to spare. Some of the celebrations when a wicket was taken have never been witnessed by a WACA crowd. After claiming an LBW, Richard Stearman performed a Klinsmann type dive in mid-wicket before his five team-mates piled on top of him. It was definitely not cricket! At the same time, the real Ashes series was beginning in England.

WOLVES AT THE WACA

FA CUP FINAL 1896

Three years after their 1893 FA Cup victory over Everton, Wolves made it through to the final once again, this time at Crystal Palace where they met Sheffield Wednesday. The Owls were a goal to the good inside two minutes when Fred Spiksley beat Bill Tennant in the Wanderers' goal. On 10 minutes left-winger David Black hooked a shot home to level matters but Spiksley was to have the last word, eight minutes later, when he ran from a seemingly off-side position to score what proved to be the winning goal. The crowd of 48,836 paid gate receipts of £1,824.

Round/scorers	Opponents/venue	Score
Round 1	Notts County (h)	2-2
Malpass, Henderson		
Replay	Notts County (a)	4-3
Beats, Wood 2, Black		
Round 2	Liverpool (h)	2-0
Owen, Wood		
Round 3	Stoke City (h)	3-0
Malpass, Tonks, Henderson		
Semi-final	Derby County (Perry Barr, Birmingham)	2-1
Malpass, Tonks		
Final	Sheffield Wednesday (Crystal Palace)	1-2
Black		

Wolves 1896 FA Cup Final team: Tennant, Baugh, Dunn, Griffiths, Malpass, Owen, Tonks, Henderson, Beats, Wood, Black.

A WATCHFUL EYE

Manchester United boss Alex Ferguson was a regular visitor to Molineux in the 1990s. Sadly, only one of the occasions was for a game between Wolves and the Reds – and that was for a friendly in 1994. The reason for his attendance was to watch his son Darren play. The midfielder joined Wolves from United in January 1994 and, by the time he left to join Sparta Rotterdam on a free transfer five years later, Ferguson junior had played one game short of 150 times for Wolves.

A BAD FINISH

After 33 seasons and 1,389 games, the curtain came down on Wolves' stay in the top-flight of English football with a 3-1 home defeat against Liverpool on a Monday evening in April 1965. And to make matters worse, the reversal came with the Merseysiders fielding a reserve side as an FA Cup final appearance at Wembley against Leeds United lay just five days away. Only 13,839 turned up to watch the last rites and just one of the Liverpool team, Geoff Strong, was included in the 11 that won the cup that following weekend.

TWENTY-ONE UP FOR TED

For Ted Farmer, Saturday January 21, 1961, proved to be a very special day in more ways than one. That 21st day of the month, the striker scored his 21st goal in what was his 21st senior appearance. It was a fitting way for him to celebrate his 21st birthday.

A BUSY TIME

In the season of 1987/88, Wolves played 61 competitive games – 46 in the League, three in the FA Cup, four in the League Cup and eight in the Sherpa Van Trophy. Goalkeeper Mark Kendall and striker Andy Mutch played in all 61 as Wanderers captured the Fourth Division title and the Sherpa Van Trophy.

FRED THE FIRST

The season of 1965/66 finally saw the introduction of substitutes in League football. In those early days just one man was named on the bench and he could only be used in the case of an injury. Wolves were 13 matches into the campaign when Fred Goodwin became the first man to appear as a substitute for the club. He was a 47th-minute replacement for Ernie Hunt in a home game against Middlesbrough. Wolves were to use the new ruling to their advantage a further five times that season with Ken Knighton coming on as 12th man three times and David Woodfield twice.

PENALTY FIRST

John Heath may have only played 12 games for Wolves, all in the 1891/92 season, but one of the four goals he scored during the campaign was to be written into football folklore. Playing against Accrington at Molineux in September 1891, he became the first player to convert a penalty in League football.

NEUTRAL AT MOLINEUX

Since the war, Molineux has hosted six FA Cup second replays and one third replay, all in the fifties and sixties. The first was a sixth round clash between Second Division Birmingham City and top-flight Tottenham Hotspur in 1953 with the Londoners emerging as 1-0 winners in front of a crowd of 50,801. The following year Blackpool finally saw off the threat of Luton Town by 2-0 after three drawn games. Another healthy attendance, 36,554, watched Stoke City beat Aston Villa 2-0 in a third round replay in 1958 and Crystal Palace won 4-1 in a second round, second replay, against Shrewsbury Town in December of that year. Stoke returned in 1961 having played out two goalless fourth round draws against Aldershot Town. The Potters emerged victorious at the third time of asking by 3-0. Just 2,052 watched the fourth qualifying round tie which saw Hereford United overcome Hinckley Athletic by 3-2 in 1965. The final time that Molineux was used as a neutral venue was for a quarter-final between Everton and Manchester City with the Merseysiders coming out on top by 2-0 in front of 27,948 in March 1966.

FIRST AND LAST

South African defender Eddie Stuart scored on his debut after Stan Cullis had drafted him in as an emergency striker against West Bromwich Albion in April 1952 – injuries had left the manager short of options up front. His goal was scant consolation for the Wolves fans in the 48,000 crowd at Molineux as the Baggies ran out 4-1 winners. But it was a goal that Eddie wouldn't forget as, in the 321 further games he was to play in the club's colours, he was destined never to find the net again.

FALSE DAWN

Hopes were high when Wolves began the 1981/82 season with a 1-0 Molineux victory over mighty Liverpool – Mick Matthews heading the solitary goal. But it was to prove a false dawn with just four goals and one win coming from the next 11 matches. Wolves went out of the League Cup and FA Cup at the first hurdles and were relegated at the end of the campaign. And worse was to follow with the club going into liquidation in the summer of 1982.

MANAGERS

1885-1922	Jack Addenbroke
1922-1924	George Jobey
1924-1926	Albert Hoskins
1926-1927	Fred Scotchbrook
1927-1944	Major Frank Buckley
1944-1948	Ted Vizard
1948-1964	Stan Cullis
1964-1965	Andy Beattie
1965-1968	Ronnie Allen
1968-1976	Bill McGarry
1976-1978	Sammy Chung
1978-1982	John Barnwell
1982	Ian Greaves
1982-1984	Graham Hawkins
1984-1985	Tommy Docherty
1985	Sammy Chapman
1985	Bill McGarry
1985-1986	Sammy Chapman
1986	Brian Little
1986-1994	Graham Turner
1994-1995	Graham Taylor
1995-1998	Mark McGhee
1998-2000	Colin Lee
2001-2004	Dave Jones
2004-2006	Glenn Hoddle
2006-	Mick McCarthy

FIRST FROM A TWELFTH MAN

Canadian Les Wilson was the first man to score for Wolves after coming on as a substitute. The game was against Everton at Goodison Park in September 1967 but, unfortunately, his goal made no difference to the outcome of the game with the final scoreline being 4-2 in favour of the Merseyside team.

IWAN'S DAY

When Wolves met West Bromwich Albion at The Hawthorns in September 1996, Welsh international Iwan Roberts became the first player from either side to score a hat-trick in a Black Country derby at the home of the Baggies. Roberts was on target twice in the opening 28 minutes with Steve Bull also hitting the net. Although Albion pulled one back before the break, Roberts completed his treble in the 53rd minute with Wolves finishing the game as 4-2 victors. Winger Steve Froggatt had an assist in all four of the Molineux team's goals.

GATES CLOSED

The highest attendance for a game at Molineux came shortly before the Second World War in a fifth round FA Cup tie against Liverpool. The ground was bursting at the seams as 61,315 packed in to watch Stan Burton, Dickie Dorsett, Alex McIntosh and Dennis Westcott score in a 4-1 victory. More Merseyside opposition followed in the quarter-final with Westcott netting both goals in a 2-0 triumph over Everton in front of another huge crowd just 1,760 lower than in the previous round.

INTO THE CUP

Wolves first participated in the FA Cup in October 1883 when John Griffiths and Jack Brodie each grabbed a brace in a 4-1 win over Long Eaton Rangers. Brodie also grabbed two in the next round – an away game at Wednesbury Old Athletic who went through thanks to a 4-2 scoreline.

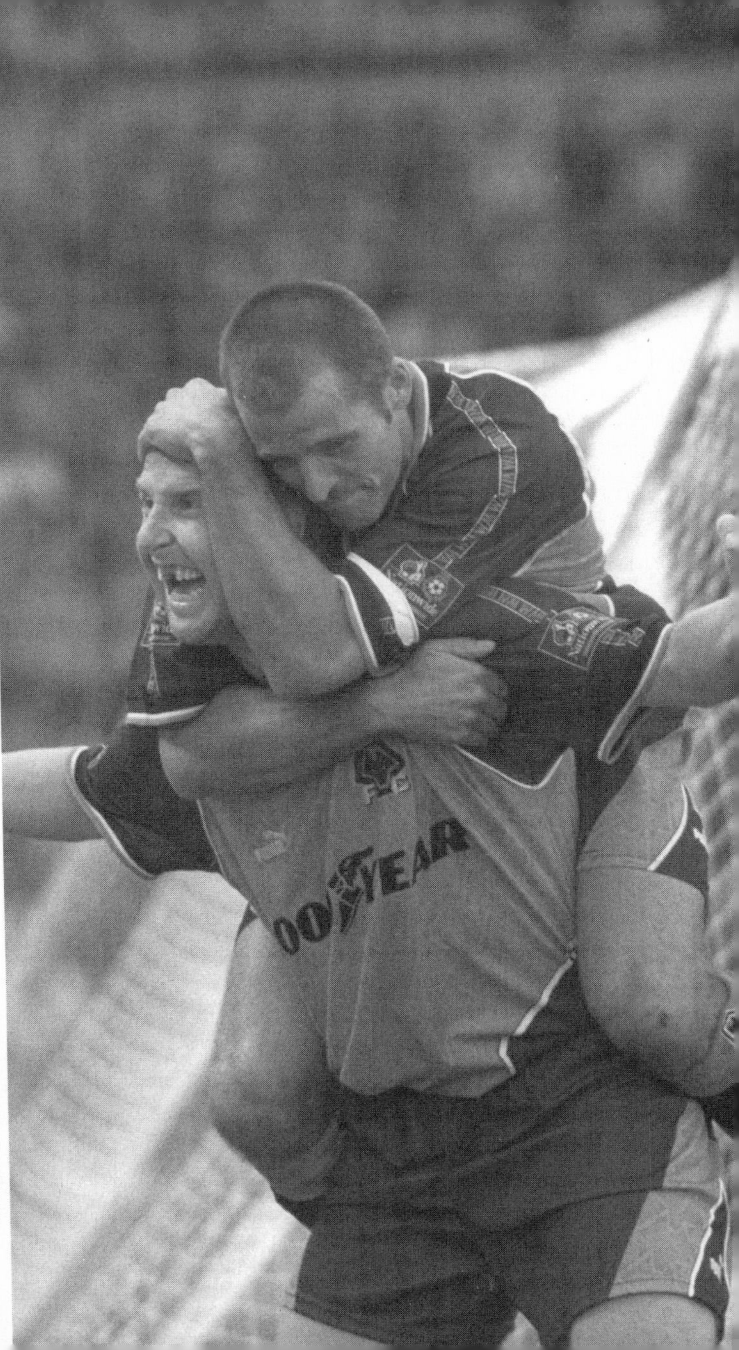

IWAN ROBERTS: HAWTHORNS HAT-TRICK

OOPS!

An electric atmosphere greeted the players of Wolves and Coventry City as they ran out for a sixth round FA Cup tie in front of a 50,000 crowd at Molineux in March 1973. But, during the pre-match kick-in, home favourite Derek Dougan fell to the ground after a shot from substitute Steve Kindon struck the Northern Ireland international on the back of the head, knocking him out. The kick-off was delayed whilst Dougan recovered as an embarrassed Kindon made his way to the bench – doubtless avoiding eye contact with his manager, Bill McGarry. Wolves won the game 2-1 with Dougan's flicked header setting up the opening goal for John Richards.

ENGLAND AT MOLINEUX

There have been four full England internationals played at Molineux, the first of which took place as long ago as March 1891, when Wolves favourites William Rose and Jack Brodie played their part in a 6-1 beating of Ireland. Twelve years later another England v Ireland clash saw another England win, this time 4-0 with the only Wanderers player involved being Tom Baddeley who, like Rose, was a goalkeeper. Two Wolves players were involved when England met Wales in 1936 – but not for the home country. Dai Richards and Bryn Jones donned the red and white of Wales and Jones got one of his team's goals in a 2-1 win over the English. In a World Cup qualifier in December 1956, Billy Wright captained England to a 5-2 victory over Denmark in front of a 54,083 crowd at Molineux. The Manchester United duo of Tommy Taylor and Duncan Edwards scored the five goals between them with Taylor grabbing a hat-trick and Edwards a brace.

FA CUP FINAL 1908

It was an unusually cold day when Wolves met Newcastle United to contest the FA Cup Final at the Crystal Palace on April 25, 1908. Snow had fallen on the morning of a game that the First Division Geordies were hot favourites to win against a Wanderers team stuck in mid-table of Division Two. But one of the biggest shocks in the competition's history was to take place that afternoon. Newcastle, with several internationals in their line-up, were the reigning League Champions. Wolves fielded an all-English side, eight of whom were natives of Wolverhampton or the surrounding district. Five minutes before the interval, the Reverend Kenneth Hunt shot home from 25 yards to give Wolves the lead and, just three minutes later, George Hedley added a second. Although Jimmy Howie pulled one back for the Tynesiders in the 73rd minute, Billy Harrison, whose wife had given birth to triplets shortly before the game, sealed matters with a fine individual goal five minutes from the end. Four of the 22 players involved in the final had a surname with the initial H and they each scored a goal in the game. Ten of the Wolves team played in the seven matches of the Cup run with Walter Radford taking over the number 10 shirt from Percy Corbett who took part in the two games against Bradford City. Upon returning to Wolverhampton, a huge crowd had gathered at the High Level Station and they carried the players shoulder high to the nearby Victoria Hotel where a celebratory reception lay in wait.

Round/scorers	Opponents/venue	Score
Round 1	Bradford City (a)	1-1
Shelton		
Replay	Bradford City (h)	1-0
Hedley		
Round 2	Bury (h)	2-0
Radford 2		
Round 3	Swindon Town (h)	2-0
Harrison, Hedley		
Round 4	Stoke City (a)	1-0
Radford		
Semi-Final	Southampton (Stamford Bridge)	2-0
Hedley, Radford		
Final	Newcastle United (Crystal Palace)	3-1
Hunt, Hedley, Harrison		

Wolves 1908 FA Cup Final team: Lunn, Jones, Collins, Hunt, Wooldridge, Bishop, Harrison, Shelton, Hedley, Radford, Pedley.

FA CUP FINAL 1921

It was something of a surprise when Wanderers made it through to the FA Cup Final in 1921. After finishing the first post-war season in a disappointing 19th place in the Second Division, there was little improvement in the following term with the side struggling in the lower half of the table. But the cup campaign was a different matter with Wolves beating top-flight opposition in the shape of Derby County and Everton on the way to the final at Stamford Bridge where First Division Tottenham Hotspur lay in wait. The circumstances were similar to those of 13 years earlier when a Molineux team from the second tier had shocked the football world by beating high-flying Newcastle. This time, however, there was no happy ending for Jack Addenbrooke's side. The teams were presented to King George V on a muddy pitch as rain poured down on the 72,805 crowd. Goalkeeper Noel George made several fine saves in the first half keeping the Spurs forwards at bay but he was finally beaten by Jimmy Dimmock's low shot, eight minutes into the second half. Sammy Brooks went close for Wolves but Dimmock's effort proved to be the only goal of the game.

Round/scorers	Opponents/venue	Score
Round 1	Stoke City (h)	3-2
Burrill, Edmonds 2		
Round 2	Derby County (a)	1-1
Whiteman og		
Replay	Derby County (h)	1-0
Richards		
Round 3	Fulham (a)	1-0
Potts		
Round 4	Everton (a)	1-0
Edmonds		
Semi-Final	Cardiff City (Anfield)	0-0
SF Replay	Cardiff City (Old Trafford)	3-0
Richards, Edmonds, Brooks		
Final	Tottenham Hotspur (Stamford Bridge)	0-1

Wolves 1921 FA Cup Final team: George, Woodward, Marshall, Gregory, Hodnett, Riley, Lea, Burrill, Edmonds, Potts, Brooks.

SHOOT-OUT DRAMA

Wolves were as good as out of the 1995 FA Cup when, in a fourth round replay against Sheffield Wednesday at Molineux, the Owls took a 3-0 advantage in the penalty shoot-out that was held after extra-time couldn't separate the teams. The game had finished at one-all following 90 minutes with David Kelly's early goal being cancelled out by Mark Bright in the 56th minute. Bright successfully began the shoot-out but the normally reliable Andy Thompson put his kick over the bar. Guy Whittingham converted to put the visitors two up before Robbie Dennison saw his shot saved by Kevin Pressman. When Pressman himself lashed home Wednesday's third kick it meant that one more miss for Wolves, or one more conversion from the Yorkshire side, would have ended the tie. Gordon Cowans finally gave the home support something to cheer by beating Pressman as did Kelly after Andy Pearce had shot over with his effort. But the stadium really sparked to life when Paul Jones saved from Chris Bart-Williams leaving John de Wolf to level matters at three penalties each. And after Jones had dived to save Chris Waddle's tame effort, Don Goodman strode up to rifle the ball into the roof of the net and give Wolves a victory that had looked highly unlikely a few moments earlier. Goalkeeper Jones was the hero of the first game at Hillsborough when he saved a Bart-Williams spot-kick controversially awarded just three minutes from the end of a game that was to finish goalless.

LEAGUE RUNNERS-UP

Wolves have endured the agony of finishing second in the Football League Championship five times. In 1938 they finished a point behind Arsenal and, 12 months later, there was a four-point gap between them and champions Everton. In 1950, Portsmouth took the honours by the narrowest of margins – goal average – despite Wolves' 6-1 beating of Birmingham at Molineux on the final day of the season. On the same afternoon, on the south coast, Pompey hammered Aston Villa 5-1. In 1955, Chelsea had a four-point margin at the top, and five years later, Burnley won it by a single point.

YOUNGEST WOLF

Winger Jimmy Mullen became the youngest player to don the old gold and black in a first class match when he made his debut against Leeds United at the age of 16 years and 43 days in February 1939. Despite losing six years of his career through the Second World War he still made 486 appearances scoring 112 goals for Wolves – his only club. Newcastle-born Jimmy also made 89 wartime appearances for the club and, after he retired from the game in 1959, he opened a sports shop in Wolverhampton. Cameron Buchanan was only 14 years and 57 days old when he played for Wolves in a wartime derby against West Bromwich in September 1942.

TWO NUMBER ONES

A victory international between England and Wales took place at West Bromwich in October 1945. And Wolves supplied the goalkeepers for both sides with Bert Williams between the sticks for England and Cyril Sidlow for the Welsh. The crowd of 54,611 at The Hawthorns witnessed a win for Wales with Aubrey Powell of Leeds United getting the only goal of the game.

WAR CUP WINNERS

Wolves captured the Wartime League Cup in 1942, beating Sunderland in the two-legged final. The four hurdles overcome on the way to the final, each played on a home and away basis, saw Wolves beating Chester City 4-1 on aggregate, Manchester United 6-5 on aggregate, Manchester City 2-1 on aggregate and, in the semi-final, West Bromwich 7-0 on aggregate. In the first leg of the final, at Roker Park, the sides shared four goals with Dennis Westcott netting twice for the visitors. There were 43,038 at Molineux for the return and they witnessed a 4-1 home win to give Wolves the Cup on a 6-3 aggregate. Jack Rowley with two, Westcott and Frank Broome were the home scorers. A week later, on June 6, Wolves travelled to Stamford Bridge for a challenge match against the London League Cup winners, Brentford. Jimmy Mullen notched Wolves' goal in a one-all draw.

JIMMY MULLEN: A YOUTHFUL START AT MOLINEUX

FIRST PROMOTION

After the disastrous campaign of 1922/23, when Wolves slipped to the bottom tier of the Football League, the team bounced back in fine fashion to achieve their first promotion by clinching the Championship of the Third Division (North). Under the managership of George Jobey, Wanderers lost just three League games all season and although they finished only a single point ahead of runners-up Rochdale, there was a nine-point gap between first spot and the third place occupied by Chesterfield. Goalkeeper Noel George kept 23 clean sheets and the biggest win of the campaign was a 7-1 triumph at Ashington.

FOOTBALL LEAGUE DIVISION THREE NORTH

		Pl	W	D	L	F	A	W	D	L	F	A	Pts
1	WOLVES	42	18	3	0	51	10	6	12	3	25	17	63
2	Rochdale	42	17	4	0	40	8	8	8	5	20	18	62
3	Chesterfield	42	16	4	1	54	15	6	6	9	16	24	54
4	Rotherham United	42	16	3	2	46	13	7	3	11	24	30	52
5	Bradford PA	42	17	3	1	50	12	4	7	10	19	31	52
6	Darlington	42	16	5	0	51	19	4	3	14	19	34	48
7	Southport	42	13	7	1	30	10	3	7	11	14	32	46
8	Ashington	42	14	4	3	41	21	4	4	13	18	40	44
9	Doncaster Rovers	42	13	4	4	41	17	2	8	11	18	36	42
10	Wigan Borough	42	12	5	4	39	15	2	9	10	16	38	42
11	Grimsby Town	42	11	9	1	30	7	3	4	14	19	40	41
12	Tranmere Rovers	42	11	5	5	32	21	2	10	9	19	39	41
13	Accrington Stanley	42	12	5	4	35	21	4	3	14	13	40	40
14	Halifax Town	42	11	4	6	26	17	4	6	11	16	42	40
15	Durham City	42	12	5	4	40	23	3	4	14	19	37	39
16	Wrexham	42	8	11	2	24	12	2	7	12	13	32	38
17	Walsall	42	10	5	6	31	20	4	3	14	13	39	36
18	New Brighton	42	9	9	3	28	10	2	4	15	12	43	35
19	Lincoln City	42	8	8	5	29	22	2	4	15	19	37	32
20	Crewe Alexandra	42	6	7	8	20	24	1	6	14	12	34	27
21	Hartlepools United	42	5	7	9	22	24	2	4	15	11	46	25
22	Barrow	42	7	7	7	25	24	1	2	18	10	56	25

UNITED COMEBACKS

Wolves have met Manchester United five times in FA Cup ties at Molineux and in three of those games the Old Trafford side conceded a two-goal advantage to Wanderers before, on each occasion, coming back to win. In March 1964, after two Hugh McIlmoyle goals inside the first 15 minutes of a sixth round tie, Wolves were looking good for a place in the last four of the competition. But Denis Law started United's comeback in first-half injury time before David Herd, George Best (directly from a corner), Pat Crerand and Law again ruined the night for the home supporters. Peter Knowles' late strike was a mere consolation. A year later, this time in the fifth round, two Terry Wharton penalties with only nine minutes gone put Wolves in the driving seat. Law, once again, spoiled the party when he scored two goals to level matters before Best and Herd confirmed that it was United who were going through. In a 1976 sixth round replay, Steve Kindon and John Richards put Wolves two up by the midway stage of the first half before goals from Stuart Pearson and Jimmy Greenhoff took the game into extra-time when Sammy McIlroy grabbed the winner.

A STRANGE CELEBRATION

When Wolves travelled to Lincoln City in May 1986, they had already been condemned to relegation. But, however minor, there was still a prize on offer – that of not finishing bottom of the Third Division. In those dark days Wolves had finished the previous two campaigns as the bottom team of the First and then Second Divisions. But, thanks to goals from Andy Mutch, Dean Edwards and Jon Purdie, the visitors enjoyed a narrow 3-2 victory to lift themselves off the bottom. Then came a 24-hour wait for Swansea's home game with Derby County to take place. The Swans, like Wolves already doomed to the drop, needed a point from the game to avoid the wooden spoon but the Rams were 3-0 winners. A day earlier the small band of around 200 travelling Wolves fans had celebrated the 11th win of the campaign on the open Sincil Bank terraces despite the heavy rain that was falling and the realisation that bottom-tier football awaited them after the summer break.

BACK AGAIN

It proved to be a long wait, 22 seasons in all, but Wolves finally made it back to the top-flight of English football when they won the Second Division Championship in 1932. Boosted by the goals of Billy Hartill, Walter Bottrill and Charlie Phillips, the side made Molineux something of a fortress recording 17 wins and three draws in the 21 games played there that season, Stoke City being the only team to leave with two points. A club record 115 goals were scored – 71 of them at Molineux – where just 11 were conceded and three times during the campaign Major Frank Buckley's men hit seven; against Port Vale, Manchester United and Oldham Athletic.

FOOTBALL LEAGUE DIVISION TWO

		Pl	W	D	L	F	A	W	D	L	F	A	Pts
1	WOLVES	42	17	3	1	71	11	7	5	9	44	38	56
2	Leeds United	42	12	5	4	36	22	10	5	6	42	32	54
3	Stoke City	42	14	6	1	47	19	5	8	8	22	29	52
4	Plymouth Argyle	42	14	4	3	69	29	6	5	10	31	37	49
5	Bury	42	13	4	4	44	21	8	3	10	26	37	49
6	Bradford PA	42	17	2	2	44	18	4	5	12	28	45	49
7	Bradford City	42	10	7	4	53	26	6	6	9	27	35	45
8	Tottenham Hotspur	42	11	6	4	58	37	5	5	11	29	41	43
9	Millwall	42	13	3	5	43	21	4	6	11	18	40	43
10	Charlton Athletic	42	11	5	5	38	28	6	4	11	23	38	43
11	Nottingham Forest	42	13	4	4	49	27	3	6	12	28	45	42
12	Manchester United	42	12	3	6	44	31	5	5	11	27	41	42
13	Preston North End	42	11	6	4	37	25	5	4	12	38	52	42
14	Southampton	42	10	5	6	39	30	7	2	12	27	47	41
15	Swansea City	42	12	4	5	45	22	4	3	14	28	53	39
16	Notts County	42	10	4	7	43	30	3	8	10	32	45	38
17	Chesterfield	42	11	3	7	43	33	2	8	11	21	53	37
18	Oldham Athletic	42	10	4	7	41	34	3	6	12	21	50	36
19	Burnley	42	7	8	6	36	36	6	1	14	23	51	35
20	Port Vale	42	8	4	9	30	33	5	3	13	28	56	33
21	Barnsley	42	8	7	6	35	30	4	2	15	20	61	33
22	Bristol City	42	4	7	10	22	37	2	4	15	17	41	23

QUICK CHANGE

Wolves signed veteran inside forward Dave Burnside from Crystal Palace on the morning of Tuesday September 7, 1966. The teams were set to meet at Molineux that evening and Burnside's name appeared in the Palace line-up in the programme for the game. That night he replaced Peter Knowles in the Wanderers team in a game that finished at one-all. The scorer for Wolves? Yes, it was David Burnside. He began his career with West Bromwich before moves to Southampton and Palace. After an 18-month stay at Molineux, during which time he played 40 games and scored five goals, Burnside moved on to Plymouth and Bristol City before winding up his League career with Colchester United.

ALL SQUARE FOR EDDIE

Tough tackling defender Eddie Clamp won four caps playing for England and, whilst he could have claimed to have been unbeaten in his international career, he couldn't claim to be a winner either with all four games finishing as draws. After making his debut in the one-all draw with USSR in Moscow, he then featured in three of England's four games in the 1958 World Cup Finals in Sweden. After another meeting with the USSR, this time with a 2-2 result, Walter Winterbottom's men held eventual winners Brazil to a goalless draw in Gothenburg. The final game of Clamp's quartet was another 2-2 draw – against Austria in Boras. A product of Wolves' nursery club, Wath Wanderers, he was to make 241 appearances for the club scoring 25 goals between 1954 and 1961 when he left to join Arsenal.

FRIENDLY DEBUT

An injury to Roy Swinbourne presented 20-year-old Jimmy Murray with his debut in the high profile friendly against Moscow Dynamo in November 1955. A packed Molineux crowd witnessed the striker creating a goal for Jimmy Mullen before hitting the bar himself. Murray went on to make 299 League and Cup appearances for Wolves, scoring an impressive total of 166 times.

BEATEN BY THE BUSBY BABES

The FA Youth Cup was first contested in the season of 1952/53 and Wolves made it through to the Final in impressive fashion winning six games without conceding a goal. The Molineux youngsters started the campaign with a 5-0 win at non-League Wellington and followed that up by beating West Bromwich 2-0 at Molineux. Another 5-0 victory, this time at St Andrew's against Birmingham, was followed by a 6-0 home hammering of Doncaster Rovers. In the semi-final Wolves were drawn against the works' side of biscuit manufacturers Huntley and Palmers who were beaten on an 11-0 aggregate score over two legs. Up against Manchester United in the final a rude awakening lay in wait in the first leg at Old Trafford. After six clean sheets Wolves conceded seven against the Busby Babes replying just once. The teams shared four goals in the return as United captured the trophy with a 9-3 aggregate. A year later the same clubs contested the final with United retaining the trophy in a much closer affair. The first leg at Molineux finished in a 4-4 draw with a David Pegg penalty for the Reds deciding the contest in Manchester.

NEVER-SAY-DIE WOLVES

When referee Phil Walton blew his whistle for the half-time break at Molineux in October, 2003, Wolves were 3-0 down to Midland rivals Leicester City and, to all intents and purposes, dead and buried. Les Ferdinand had twice headed home from corners and Ricky Scimeca netted a third 10 minutes before the break to put the game seemingly out of Wolves' reach. Colin Cameron pulled one back seven minutes after the resumption then, when the Scottish midfielder converted a penalty in the 59th minute, the unlikely suddenly started to look possible. And just eight minutes later the stadium erupted as Alex Rae's superb header beat Ian Walker in the Foxes' goal to level matters. The transformation of the game was complete five minutes from the end when Henri Camara converted from close-range to spark joyous celebrations both on and off the pitch as three precious Premier League points were gained. Wolves also made a similar comeback in November 1956, when Preston North End were the visitors to Molineux. A Harry Hooper hat-trick and a Bobby Mason goal saw Wanderers home.

COLIN CAMERON CONVERTS A PENALTY AS WOLVES HIT BACK AGAINST LEICESTER CITY IN 2003

EIGHT FOR JACK

Manchester United centre forward Jack Rowley was an occasional guest for Wolves during the war years and in a Football League North match against Derby County in November 1942, he went on a one-man demolition job. The Rams were humbled 8-1 in front of the 3,218 spectators that were sprinkled around Molineux and every one of those eight goals was scored by Jack Rowley. When the teams met in the return fixture at the Baseball Ground a week later, County got their revenge with a 3-1 win against a Rowley-less Wolves side.

LATE FINISH

The post-war season of 1946/47 was due to be completed by April 26. But the severe winter weather that gripped the country in 1947 meant that many fixtures were wiped out. No games were played at Molineux in February. Indeed, the only game involving Wolves that month was at Elland Road where a Dennis Westcott goal proved enough to beat Leeds United. At the start of May Wolves still had five fixtures to complete – the last of which, against Liverpool, took place on the final day of the month.

FLOODLIT FIRST

After catching the eye of the football world with their exploits against top foreign opposition in floodlit friendlies, Wolves also grabbed the headlines with their first League game under lights at Molineux. In the penultimate home game of the 1955/56 campaign, Bill Slater – with two, Peter Broadbent, Jimmy Murray and Dennis Wilshaw – were on target in a 5-1 rout of Tottenham Hotspur. Some eight weeks earlier, Portsmouth had become the first team in England to stage a floodlit League match when they entertained Newcastle United at Fratton Park. A new, taller and brighter set of lights made their debut at Molineux in October 1957. Broadbent – with two – and Murray were again on the mark. The other goal that night was scored by Ron Flowers and again the opposition was provided by Spurs who this time went down by 4-0. The original lights were sold on to Blackpool.

FA CUP FINAL 1939

The season of 1938/39 ended in heartbreak for Wolves and their legions of supporters with the team missing out on a first League Championship by just two points, and then failing in the FA Cup Final at Wembley, despite being hot favourites to beat Portsmouth. The south-coast side finished as comfortable 4-1 winners as they denied Wanderers a third win in the competition. Pompey took the lead on the half-hour through former Wolf Bert Barlow and just before the break John Anderson made it two. Within a minute of the restart, Barlow struck again to all but confirm that it would be Portsmouth that would be parading the cup and, although Dickie Dorsett pulled one back in the 65th minute, Cliff Parker made it 4-1 seven minutes later to complete the scoring and send the Wolves players and fans home disappointed. Leading up to the semi-final, all four rounds were at Molineux with a record-breaking 61,315 watching the Liverpool tie and 59,545 the last eight meeting with Everton. Then followed another highest ever attendance when 76,962 packed Old Trafford to watch the semi-final against Grimsby Town. Wolves' route to the final was as follows:

Round/scorers	Opponents/venue	Score
Round 3	Bradford City (h)	3-1
McIntosh, Westcott 2		
Round 4	Leicester City (h)	5-1
Westcott 2, Dorsett, Maguire 2		
Round 5	Liverpool (h)	4-1
Burton, McIntosh, Westcott, Dorsett		
Round 6	Everton (h)	2-0
Westcott 2		
Semi-Final	Grimsby Town (Old Trafford)	5-0
Galley, Westcott 4		
Final	Portsmouth (Wembley)	1-4
Dorsett		

Wolves 1939 FA Cup Final team: Scott, Morris, Taylor, Galley, Cullis, Gardiner, Burton, McIntosh, Westcott, Dorsett, Maguire.

ELTON ON THE WING

Pop superstar Elton John failed to make an impression as a footballer when he played in the warm-up game of David Woodfield's testimonial in April 1974. Wearing the number seven shirt, he had Wolves' supporter Robert Plant (of Led Zeppelin fame) for company in the forward line of a team that contained several of the club's former greats including Jimmy Mullen, Jimmy Murray and Ron Flowers along with Woodfield himself. But the team, labelled as David Woodfield's XI, succumbed to Don Howe's X1 by 2-1.

UNDERDOG CUP WINNERS

Wolves are one of just seven teams that have won the FA Cup when not in the top-flight of English football since the Football League was formed in 1888. Tottenham Hotspur, who were then in the Southern League, were the first to achieve the feat when they beat Sheffield United in 1901 seven years before Second Division Wolves overcame hot favourites Newcastle United by 3-1 at the old Crystal Palace. The other five instances also featured Second Division winners with Barnsley beating West Bromwich in 1912, West Bromwich winning against local rivals Birmingham in 1931, Sunderland defeating Leeds in 1973, Southampton's one-goal surprise triumph against Manchester United in 1976, and West Ham's victory over Arsenal in 1980.

GAZZA IN GOLD AND BLACK

The colourful figure of Paul Gascoigne had a short spell with Wolves in October and November, 2003 when he trained with the club and played in a series of five reserve games. His inclusion in the team boosted reserve gates at Telford's Bucks Head – the home of Wanderers' second string – but he was on the losing side four times; at home to Sunderland, Blackburn and Everton, and away to West Bromwich Albion where a crowd of 3,724 turned up to watch the game at Kidderminster. He did, however, score one of Wolves' two goals in a draw against Birmingham City at Solihull Borough's ground.

CHRISTMAS CHEER

Between 1901 and 1956 Wolves played 27 matches on Christmas Day; winning thirteen times, drawing three and losing eleven. Over the 27 games, the goals for and against tally was remarkably close at 52-51. Matches were played on Christmas Day, because bumper crowds were guaranteed. The tradition was ended in the 1950s and the last time Wolves played on 25th December was against Charlton Athletic at The Valley in 1956 – a match which ended in a 2-1 defeat.

1901	Derby County (a) 1-3
1907	Gainsborough Trinity (h) 1-0
1908	Derby County (h) 1-1
1909	West Bromwich Albion (a) 1-0
1911	Leicester Fosse (a) 1-1
1912	Nottingham Forest (a) 0-2
1914	Hull City (a) 1-5
1920	Stockport County (a) 2-1
1922	Coventry City (a) 1-7
1923	Durham City (h) 2-1
1924	Chelsea (a) 0-1
1925	Oldham Athletic (a) 2-1
1926	Bradford City (h) 7-2
1928	Nottingham Forest (h) 2-3
1930	Oldham Athletic (a) 0-2
1931	Manchester United (a) 2-3
1932	Aston Villa (a) 3-1
1933	Aston Villa (a) 2-6
1934	Derby County (h) 5-1
1935	Bolton Wanderers (a) 3-0
1936	Huddersfield Town (h) 3-1
1946	Sunderland (a) 1-0
1948	Aston Villa (h) 4-0
1950	Huddersfield Town (a) 2-1
1951	Aston Villa (a) 3-3
1954	Everton (h) 1-3
1956	Charlton Athletic (a) 1-2

A BIT LATE

Wolves finished the 1905/06 season with high-scoring home victories over East Midlands opposition. After beating Notts County 6-1 on a Monday afternoon, Wanderers hit Derby County for seven without reply five days later. Championship form – certainly. But it was all too late as the team had already been condemned to relegation having won just six of the 36 games that preceded the encouraging finish to the campaign. The 99 goals conceded during the season is an unwanted club record that stands to this day and will, hopefully, never be beaten.

EXTRA-EXTRA TIME

A wartime Football League Cup game at Molineux between Wolves and Birmingham City lasted for 153 minutes before finally reaching a conclusion at 5.50pm after a three o'clock start. After 90 minutes and extra-time had failed to find a winner, or a goal, it was decided to play on until the deadlock was broken. Home full-back Bill Morris was the man who got the all-important strike finally allowing the 30,000-strong crowd to make their way home.

FA CUP FINAL 1949

Wolves didn't have an easy passage to the 1949 FA Cup Final but they thoroughly deserved the chance to visit Wembley for a second time especially after the heroics performed in the semi-final against Manchester United when Stan Cullis lost both of his full-backs. Roy Pritchard was injured in the early stages and he could only continue as a virtual 'passenger' on the left-wing. Laurie Kelly was then stretchered off to reduce Wolves to nine fit players who held on to take United to a replay which was decided by a Sammy Smyth goal. Leicester City, the surprise package of that season's competition, lay in wait at Wembley. The Foxes were struggling to avoid relegation from the Second Division but, as well as beating top-flight Birmingham and Preston in their cup run, had seen off Champions elect Portsmouth in the semi-final. City played their part in an open and entertaining final but they were up against a Wolves side in determined mood.

CELEBRATION TIME: WEMBLEY 1949

Jesse Pye opened the scoring in the 12th minute with a classic header from Johnny Hancocks' precision centre and, three minutes before the break, it was Pye again – this time with a low shot – that made it two. Leicester hit back two minutes after the interval through Mal Griffiths and they then had a 'goal' wiped out by the off-side flag. But, midway through the half, Sammy Smyth restored Wanderers' two-goal advantage with a superb solo effort. He weaved his way through the Leicester defence before finishing clinically to all but confirm Wolves' name on the trophy.

Round/scorers	Opponents/venue	Score
Round 3	Chesterfield (h)	6-0
Hancocks, Smyth 2, Pye 2, Mullen		
Round 4	Sheffield United (a)	3-0
Hancocks 2, Dunn		
Round 5	Liverpool (h)	3-1
Smyth, Dunn, Mullen		
Round 6	West Bromwich Albion (h)	1-0
Mullen		
Semi-Final	Manchester United (Hillsborough)	1-1
Smyth		
SF Replay	Manchester United (Goodison Park)	1-0
Smyth		
Final	Leicester City (Wembley)	3-1
Pye 2, Smyth		

Wolves 1949 FA Cup Final team: Williams, Pritchard, Springthorpe, Crook, Shorthouse, Wright, Hancocks, Smyth, Pye, Dunn, Mullen.

FIRST SUNDAY GAME

The local derby with Aston Villa, at Molineux in October 1983, marked the first time that Wolves had played a game on a Sunday. The match was televised live and the one-all draw, with Wayne Clarke's 52nd-minute strike cancelling out the first-half opener from former Wolf Peter Withe, realised only the third point Wolves had taken from their opening 10 League fixtures that season. A crowd of just 13,202 turned up to watch.

LEEDS LAMENT

Just 48 hours after they had won the FA Cup by beating Arsenal 1-0 at Wembley, Leeds arrived at Molineux knowing a win would give them the 1972 League Championship and, of course, the double. The gates were locked well before kick-off and it was obvious, on that Monday night, that the visitors were suffering from the effects of their efforts of the weekend. Frank Munro gave Wolves the lead shortly before the interval and, when Derek Dougan added a second midway through the second half, Leeds' hopes were diminishing rapidly. But Billy Bremner pulled one back almost immediately to set up a nerve-jangling final 20 minutes in which both sides had efforts cleared off the line, John Richards had a 'goal' disallowed and Leeds had strong penalty appeals rejected. There were four minutes of added time but Wolves held on for the win.

LAST TERRACES

On May Day in 1993, Wolves' final home game of the season, against Millwall, was the last where spectators could stand to watch at Molineux. The South Bank was the only terraced part of the ground remaining with the Waterloo Road enclosure and North Bank, which were closed in the wake of the Bradford fire disaster in 1985, having been replaced respectively by the Billy Wright and Stan Cullis Stands. A crowd of 12,054 watched the Millwall match with Shaun Bradbury hitting two and Mark Burke the other in a 3-1 win.

ONE OF THE OLDEST

Only five Football League and Premiership clubs have played at the same home ground longer than Wolves have at Molineux. Burnley and Preston North End both played in the 1870s at Turf Moor and Deepdale respectively, whilst Chesterfield started at Saltergate in 1884, Bury at Gigg Lane in 1885 and Barnsley at Oakwell in 1887. Sheffield United first used Bramall Lane in the same season, 1889/90, as Wolves did Molineux.

DOUBLE KICK-OFF

When Wolves met Stoke at Molineux in August, 1963, it probably went unnoticed by many of the 43,217 crowd that referee J K Parr of Blackpool allowed the home side to kick off at the start of each half. Ted Farmer and Chris Crowe scored Wolves' goals in the 2-1 win.

CHARITY SHIELD 1949

FA Cup winners Wolves met League Champions Portsmouth to contest the Charity Shield in October 1949. The game was played at Highbury in front of a 35,000 crowd. It was the first time that either team had played for the Shield and, after a one-all draw, they were to hold the trophy for six months each with Pompey taking it back to Fratton Park after the game as the first to display it. Both goals in the game were controversial with Portsmouth's opener on the half-hour mark being scored by Duggie Reid who looked to be at least three yards off-side when he took a short pass from Ike Clarke with the Wolves defence hesitating, expecting the lineman's flag. The equalising goal came as the second half reached its midway point when full-back Harry Ferrier was adjudged to have handled a Johnny Hancocks drive. Such was the ferocity of the shot, it was difficult to tell whether it was hands or not and indeed if it was deliberate in any case. But the referee pointed to the spot and Hancocks duly despatched the ball past Ernie Butler in the Pompey goal. Wolves: Parsons, Kelly, Springthorpe, Russell, Shorthouse, Crook, Hancocks, Smyth, Pye, Dunn, Mullen.

TOGETHER TO WEMBLEY

Ten players played in all six games of Wolves' FA Cup campaign in 1939. Alex Scott, Bill Morris, Frank Taylor, Tom Galley, Stan Cullis, Joe Gardiner, Alex McIntosh, Dennis Westcott, Dickie Dorsett and Teddy Maguire played from the third round to the final with Jimmy Mullen standing in for Stan Burton at the quarter and semi-final stages. Burton returned for the final which was won by underdogs Portsmouth. Westcott, who had found the net in each of the rounds scoring a total of 11 goals, failed to hit the target at Wembley.

STEVE KINDON PUTS WOLVES ONE UP AGAINST MANCHESTER UNITED IN A 1976 FA CUP SIXTH ROUND REPLAY

JUST THE ONCE

There are 12 clubs that Wolves have met just once in home and away League fixtures during the course of a season. They are: Accrington Stanley (1923/24), Ashington (1923/24), Barrow (1923/24), Burton United (1906/07), Chester City (1988/89), Durham City (1923/24), Mansfield Town (1988/89), New Brighton (1923/24), Scarborough (1987/88), Southport (1923/24), Wigan Borough (1923/24) and York City (1985/86).

BAPTISM OF FIRE

After the 19-year wait for the return of top-flight football to Wolverhampton, things didn't go quite to plan in the opening home and away fixtures of the club's debut in the Premiership come August 2003. On the first day of the campaign at Ewood Park, Blackburn Rovers rattled in five goals with Wolves' solitary effort, the club's first in the Premier League, coming from Steffen Iversen. The following weekend Charlton Athletic were the visitors to Molineux and they scored four without reply. It wasn't until the eighth game of the season, when Colin Cameron's goal proved enough to beat Manchester City at Molineux, that Wolves registered their first win.

BRIGHTON BOGEY

Other than for a friendly, Wolves' first meeting with Brighton & Hove Albion came in September 1969, in a third round League Cup tie at the Goldstone Ground. Two goals from Hugh Curran and one from David Woodfield secured a 3-2 win. In 1979, this time in the FA Cup, Wolves won again by the same score at the same venue. But the League games between the clubs were to prove a different matter with the Seagulls winning the first encounter just before Christmas 1979, by 3-1 at Molineux, and then the next eight games between the sides. Wolves finally broke the hoodoo, at the 10th attempt, with a draw at the Goldstone in December 1989. The elusive first win came two years and four games later when Mark Burke and Andy Mutch found the back of the net in a 2-0 Molineux triumph.

HARD LUCK BILL

Manchester City centre forward Bill McAdams must have been cursing his luck following his side's fixture against Wolves at Maine Road in September 1959. For Bill hit a hat-trick and yet still finished on the losing side. He scored City's second goal in only the sixth minute and then an equaliser after Norman Deeley, Bill Slater and Jimmy Murray had turned the game around. Shortly before the break, Murray restored Wolves' lead only for McAdams to tie things up again five minutes after the interval. Slater – playing as an inside forward – and Micky Lill made the final score 6-4 to Wanderers. Lill's goal came in the 67th minute and the only real surprise to the 43,000 crowd that day was that the final quarter of the game produced no further goals.

GEORGE IN GOLD AND BLACK

The gifted figure of George Best once guested for Wolves – the team he supported as a youngster. He wore the number seven shirt in Mike Bailey's testimonial game against West Bromwich Albion at Molineux in October 1976. Willie Carr had already given Wolves the lead when Best struck three minutes before the interval as he held off two defenders after a 40-yard run before firing past John Osborne in the Baggies goal. But, on the hour mark, he had the crowd on their feet with an even better strike – a chip over the keeper and into the net from the tightest of angles despite the close attentions of a defender. The final score in the testimonial, which was watched by a 19,733 crowd, was 3-0.

CHAMPIONS AT LAST

After so many near things, the season of 1953/54 saw Wolves finally capture the First Division Championship. They didn't make a particularly auspicious start to a campaign that began with three away games and saw defeats at Burnley (4-1) and Sunderland (3-2) sandwiching a 4-0 Maine Road mauling of Manchester City. But then the side 'clicked into gear' and in the 18 matches that followed they won 13 and drew five. One of the wins was against Chelsea when each of the five forwards scored in an 8-1 massacre of the Stamford Bridge men. Wolves went into the final game of the term knowing that only a 7-0 home defeat at the hands of Spurs could cost them the title. As it was, Jimmy Mullen centres – in the 19th and 68th minutes – were duly headed home by Roy Swinbourne to ensure there were to be no muted celebrations at the final whistle. The 96 League goals scored by Wolves were shared by just seven players. Dennis Wilshaw top scored with 26, Johnny Hancocks and Swinbourne weighed in with 24 each, Peter Broadbent scored 12, Mullen seven, Bill Slater two and Les Smith one. A total of 22 players were used by Stan Cullis during the campaign with Hancocks the only ever-present.

FOOTBALL LEAGUE DIVISION ONE

		Pl	W	D	L	F	A	W	D	L	F	A	Pts
1	WOLVES	42	16	1	4	61	25	9	6	6	35	31	57
2	West Brom. Albion	42	13	5	3	51	24	9	4	8	35	39	53
3	Huddersfield Town	42	13	6	2	45	24	7	5	9	33	37	51
4	Manchester United	42	11	6	4	41	27	7	6	8	32	31	48
5	Bolton Wanderers	42	14	6	1	45	20	4	6	11	30	40	48
6	Blackpool	42	13	6	2	43	19	6	4	11	3750		48
7	Burnley	42	16	2	3	51	23	5	2	14	27	44	46
8	Chelsea	42	12	3	6	45	26	4	9	8	29	42	44
9	Charlton Athletic	42	14	4	3	51	26	5	2	14	24	51	44
10	Cardiff City	42	12	4	5	32	27	6	4	11	19	44	44
11	Preston North End	42	12	2	7	43	24	7	3	11	44	34	43
12	Arsenal	42	8	8	5	42	37	7	5	9	33	36	43
13	Aston Villa	42	12	5	4	50	28	4	4	13	20	40	41
14	Portsmouth	42	13	5	3	53	31	1	6	14	28	58	39
15	Newcastle United	42	9	2	10	43	40	5	8	8	29	37	38
16	Tottenham Hotspur	42	11	3	7	38	33	5	2	14	27	43	37
17	Manchester City	42	10	4	7	35	31	4	5	12	27	46	37
18	Sunderland	42	11	4	6	50	37	3	4	14	31	52	36
19	Sheffield Wednesday	42	12	4	5	43	30	3	2	16	27	61	36
20	Sheffield United	42	9	5	7	43	38	2	6	13	26	52	33
21	Middlesbrough	42	6	6	9	29	35	4	4	13	31	56	30
22	Liverpool	42	7	8	6	49	38	2	2	17	19	59	28

A SAD SATURDAY

Wolves didn't have a game on Saturday February 8, 1958, for the most tragic of reasons. That day they were due to play Manchester United at Old Trafford but, two days earlier, the Lancashire club was devastated by the Munich air disaster.

CHARITY SHIELD 1954

Injuries and international call-ups meant that Wolves drafted in four reserves and West Bromwich two when the sides met at Molineux to contest the 1954 Charity Shield. But the 45,035 crowd was treated to a game regarded by many as one of the finest ever seen at the ground. Roy Swinbourne gave Wolves a 15th-minute lead before Albion, controversially, had two 'goals' disallowed short of the interval. The second half produced a goal feast which started after just a minute when Norman Deeley headed in following Johnny Hancocks' free-kick before two goals from Ronnie Allen – in the 55th and 57th minutes – squared things up. Back came Wolves and Swinbourne (65 minutes) and Hancocks (71 minutes) quickly restored the two-goal advantage. But the Baggies were not to be outdone and after Reg Ryan had made it 4-3 with a quarter of an hour remaining, Allen then completed the scoring and his hat-trick in the 83rd minute to give the clubs a share of the Shield over the 12 months that followed. Wolves: Williams, Guttridge, Shorthouse, Flowers, Russell, Clamp, Hancocks, Broadbent, Swinbourne, Deeley, Wilshaw.

RON'S EURO FIRST

England's first game in the European Championships, or European Nations Cup as it was known then, was a qualifier against France at Hillsborough in October 1962. Yvon Goujon gave the French an 8th-minute lead before the honour of scoring England's first ever goal in the competition fell to Wolves wing-half Ron Flowers. The Yorkshireman, who won his 37th cap that day, successfully converted a 57th-minute penalty. In February the following year, France made no mistake in the second leg of the tie in Paris – running out 5-2 winners. Ron remains England's most successful penalty taker with six out of six.

MATCH OF THE DAY

Wolves made their debut on *Match of the Day* during the tempestuous season of 1964/65 which ended in relegation and saw the parting of the ways for Stan Cullis and the club. The first game shown was a home victory over Tottenham Hotspur on November 14, 1964. Terry Wharton, Ray Crawford and Dick Le Flem were the scorers in a 3-1 win – just the third success of the season for Wolves. Four weeks later, highlights of a 2-1 defeat at Chelsea were broadcast. Then it wasn't until October 1965 that the team featured on the programme again when a solitary goal from Peter Knowles proved enough to beat Crystal Palace in a Second Division clash at Molineux.

POPULAR VISITORS

The following clubs achieved record attendances when Wolves were the visitors:

Blackpool: Division One; September 17, 1955 38,058
Coventry City: Division Two; April 29, 1967 51,455
Grimsby Town: FA Cup 5; February 20, 1937 31,657
Liverpool: FA Cup 4; February 2, 1952 61,905
Manchester U: FA Cup SF v Grimsby T; March 25, 1939 76,962
Walsall: Division One; January 11, 2003 11,037

BLEAK VIEW

A crowd of 31,648 didn't get good value for money when Wolves met Everton at Molineux in October 1961. Many booed and whistled when the referee allowed the game to continue in ever-thicker fog. Visibility was so bad that a linesman had to run to the bench to get attention for a player injured in the penalty area and Everton goalkeeper Albert Dunlop remained on the field for fully a minute before someone ran on to tell him that the 90 minutes were up. Everton won the game 3-0 and many were unaware that Jimmy Gabriel had scored the Merseysiders' third shortly before the end. The race meeting at nearby Dunstall Park was abandoned shortly after the 3pm race.

HANDY SWITCH

An injury to Jimmy Murray forced Stan Cullis to switch Peter Broadbent from his customary inside-right position to that of centre-forward a week before Christmas in 1959. Broadbent didn't let his manager down, scoring in a 3-1 win over Nottingham Forest at the City Ground. And then, on Boxing Day at Fratton Park, he bagged a hat-trick in Wolves' 5-3 triumph on the south coast. In the return fixture the following day, he failed to find the net. The only problem for Pompey was that Norman Deeley and Colin Booth both registered hat-tricks – along with a single strike from Des Horne – to give Wolves a 7-0 Yuletide double.

BILLY UP FOR THE CUP

From the end of the Second World War until his retirement in 1959, Billy Wright took part in every one of the 48 FA Cup games that Wolves contested in those 14 seasons. The cup highlight for Billy was undoubtedly when he hoisted the trophy at Wembley after beating Leicester City in the 1949 Final.

FIRST THREE-POINTER

Wolves' 1-0 victory over Liverpool on the opening day of the 1981/82 campaign gave the club its first three-point haul from a single game after the Football League had upped the reward for a win from two points to three in a bid to stop teams hanging on for a draw thus, hopefully, making the game of football more attractive and exciting.

JR'S THREE FROM THE BENCH

The only Wolves man to score a hat-trick after coming on as a substitute is John Richards after he had replaced Dave Wagstaffe in the 23rd minute of a fifth round FA Cup tie against Charlton Athletic in February 1976. He struck his first goal just five minutes after his introduction and found the net again in the 56th and 89th minutes to round off a 3-0 victory.

ABOUT TURN

Wolves displayed Championship form at the start of the 1949/50 campaign, winning nine and drawing three of their opening 12 games. But what followed wasn't so inspiring. The final fixture of the sequence was a one-all draw against West Bromwich and that counted as the first of a 12-game run without a win – a run comprising seven draws and five losses.

FIRST HAT-TRICK

The man honoured with scoring the first League hat-trick for Wolves is Harry Wood who achieved the feat on November 3, 1888, in a 4-1 victory over Derby County at the Dudley Road ground in the inaugural season of the Football League.

SQUEAK THE STAYER

Derek Parkin joined Wolves from Huddersfield Town in February 1968. Nicknamed Squeak by his team-mates because of the high-pitched noise he made when shouting during a game, the left-back went on to become the man who made more appearances for Wolves than any other. He took part in a grand total of 609 games for the club, 501 of which were in the League which is another record. His total would undoubtedly have been higher had an illness not caused him to miss five months of the 1972/73 season. He was a member of the League Cup winning sides in 1974 and 1980 and won a Second Division Championship medal in 1977. Capped by England at Under-23 level, he also played for the Football League team. He left Molineux to join Stoke in 1982, playing 40 times for the Potteries side before hanging up his boots.

CHAMPIONS AGAIN

Wolves made a chequered start to what was to be their second Football League Championship campaign. After losing on the opening day by a single goal at Everton, the next two games were at Molineux where Bolton and Sunderland were hammered 6-1 and 5-0 respectively. The return at Bolton finished all square at one-all and then came a 3-1 defeat at Luton's Kenilworth Road. It was then that Stan Cullis' team clicked into gear and went on an 18-match unbeaten run that saw them drop just four points along the way. There were only four defeats in the second part of the campaign – at Spurs and Blackpool, at home to Arsenal and, somewhat surprisingly on the final day of the season, against a Sheffield Wednesday side that finished at the bottom of the table. Molineux was something of a fortress with 37 out of a possible 42 points taken. Jimmy Murray finished as top scorer with 29 goals and he also found the net three times in FA Cup fixtures. The final table was as follows:

FOOTBALL LEAGUE DIVISION ONE

		Pl	W	D	L	F	A	W	D	L	F	A	Pts
1	WOLVES	42	17	3	1	60	21	11	5	5	43	26	64
2	Preston North End	42	18	2	1	63	14	8	5	8	37	37	59
3	Tottenham Hotspur	42	13	4	4	58	33	8	5	8	35	44	51
4	West Brom Albion	42	14	4	3	59	29	4	10	7	33	41	50
5	Manchester City	42	14	4	3	58	33	8	1	12	46	67	49
6	Burnley	42	16	2	3	52	21	5	3	13	28	53	47
7	Blackpool	42	11	2	8	47	35	8	4	9	33	32	44
8	Luton Town	42	13	3	5	45	22	6	3	12	24	41	44
9	Manchester United	42	10	4	7	45	31	6	7	8	40	44	43
10	Nottingham Forest	42	10	4	7	41	27	6	6	9	28	36	42
11	Chelsea	42	10	5	6	47	34	5	7	9	36	45	42
12	Arsenal	42	10	4	7	48	39	6	3	12	25	46	39
13	Birmingham City	42	8	6	7	43	37	6	5	10	33	52	39
14	Aston Villa	42	12	4	5	46	26	4	3	14	27	60	39
15	Bolton Wanderers	42	9	5	7	38	35	5	5	11	27	52	38
16	Everton	42	5	9	7	34	35	8	2	11	31	40	37
17	Leeds United	42	10	6	5	33	23	4	3	14	18	40	37
18	Leicester City	42	11	4	6	59	41	3	1	17	32	71	33
19	Newcastle United	42	6	4	11	38	42	6	4	11	35	39	32
20	Portsmouth	42	10	6	5	45	34	2	2	17	28	54	32
21	Sunderland	42	7	7	7	32	33	3	5	13	22	64	32
22	Sheffield Wednesday	42	12	2	7	45	40	0	5	16	24	52	31

SPOT ON PHIL

Phil Parkes was the hero of Wolves' UEFA Cup semi-final against Ferencvaros, the keeper saving a penalty in each leg of the tie. The first meeting of the teams came in Budapest's Nep Stadium and Wolves were 2-1 down when the home side were awarded a second spot kick of the game with 74 minutes gone. John Richards had opened the scoring before Istvan Szoke converted from the spot and then Florian Albert netted to put the Hungarians into the lead. Szoke took the second penalty, awarded like the first after hand ball by full-back Bernard Shaw, and, although Parkes went the wrong way, he managed to keep the ball out with his foot. Five minutes later Frank Munro grabbed an equaliser to nicely set up the second leg. After just 25 seconds at Molineux, Steve Daley put Wolves ahead in the tie and when Munro made it two just before the break, the final beckoned for Bill McGarry's men. But within a minute of the restart, Lajos Ku had pulled one back and when Alan Sunderland handled in the box late in the game, Szoke was presented with the chance of levelling matters on the night and in the tie overall. But he was once again denied by the outstretched leg of Parkes and Wolves withstood late pressure to move into their first European final.

DOUBLE FIGURES ON GOOD FRIDAY

Wolves achieved their record winning score in a League match when they demolished Leicester City by 10-1 on a Good Friday afternoon at Molineux in April, 1938. Even the solitary strike for the East Midlands club came from a Wolves man – Stan Cullis scoring an own-goal after a mix-up with keeper Cyril Sidlow. There was a crowd of 25,540 in the ground to witness the event and they saw Dennis Westcott open the scoring after 13 minutes. Then Dickie Dorsett netted a hat-trick in a 20-minute spell before the break. Bryn Jones and Westcott made it six shortly after the resumption before, with an hour gone, Teddy Maguire added a seventh. Cullis' mistake gave the visitors some momentary respite but, in the final seven minutes, three more home goals saw a double figure score attained. Dorsett helped himself to his fourth goal of the contest and, not wishing to be outdone, Westcott got the final two of the game to join his team-mate as a quadruple scorer.

THIRD PLACE

Wolves are one of just five teams that have finished third in the FA Cup. The idea of the two losing semi-finalists contesting third place as a pre-season game came to fruition in 1970 with Manchester United defeating Watford 2-0. Stoke beat Everton (3-2) in 1971, and Birmingham defeated Stoke 5-4 in a penalty shoot-out following a goalless draw a year later. In August 1973, Wolves met Arsenal at Highbury and, on a sunny afternoon in north London, they enjoyed a fine 3-1 victory over the Gunners. Jim McCalliog gave Wolves a 16th-minute lead with a low shot and Derek Dougan grabbed a second 10 minutes before the break. Brian Hornsby reduced the deficit shortly after the resumption but Dougan netted Wolves' third on the hour mark to complete the scoring. The winning side were awarded engraved tankards after the final whistle. Burnley beat Leicester (1-0) in 1974 – the final year of third place play-offs.

BAGGIES BLUNT GOOD RUN

The 5-2 home victory over Stoke City at Molineux in November, 1893, sparked a run that brought Wolves eight wins, a draw and a single defeat in 10 matches. From nine of the games 27 goals were scored and just six conceded which made it all the more peculiar that the defeat – at the hands of local rivals West Bromwich Albion – handed Wolves their worst League defeat at Molineux; a record that has lasted to this day. The Baggies registered eight goals without reply and they finished the season in eighth place, a point and one position better than Wolves.

FIRST TO 7000

South Korean midfielder Seol Ki Hyeon made history with his goal against Crystal Palace at Selhurst Park on December 10, 2005. It wasn't a particularly spectacular effort; a low cross that eluded everyone and crept in at the far post. But it was enough to earn a point from the trip to south London and it was also the 7,000th League goal scored by Wolves, the first team to reach the landmark figure.

SIX HITTER SAINTS

When Southampton rattled six goals beyond home keeper Matt Murray in March 2007, it was the first time that Wolves had conceded six in a home match in almost 31 years. The last team to do it, back in October 1976, was Southampton who won a Second Division fixture 6-2.

A LONELY PLACE

The Brisbane Road dressing-room must have seemed a very lonely place to Leyton Orient inside forward Gordon Ferry when Wolves visited the London venue in October 1965. Dave Wagstaffe gave Wanderers an early lead and then, with 21 minutes gone, Ferry's attempted clearance flew into the net. Worse followed for the unfortunate Ferry for 11 minutes after the break, under pressure from Peter Knowles and Terry Wharton, his attempted back-pass went straight past his goalkeeper into the goal. The final score was 3-0 in Wolves' favour.

MAGNIFICENT COMEBACK

As the 1957/58 season drew to a close, the Wolves youth team produced one of the greatest comebacks ever known in the game when they met Chelsea in that year's FA Youth Cup final. Played on a two-leg basis, the contest looked all but over when Chelsea won 5-1 at Stamford Bridge on April 29. Brian Perry had given Wolves an early lead in London but Jimmy Greaves and Mike Harrison scored before half-time to edge the home side in front. In the second half Chelsea seemed to have made the trophy theirs when Mike Block, Harrison and Barry Bridges added further goals. However, it was a different story in the return at Molineux two days later as a 17,704 crowd witnessed a phenomenal contest. Ted Farmer scored four first-half goals to level the tie on aggregate and, late in the match, Cliff Durandt struck twice to put Wolves 7-5 up. Chelsea's only reply was a goal from Greaves in the last few minutes. Wolves (first leg): Cullen, Kelly, Yates, Kirkham, Palin, Cocker, Horne, Hall, Farmer, Durandt, Perry. (Read replaced Perry as the only change in the second leg).

FULL HOUSE FOR GERRARD

All roads led to the Bucks Head when Steven Gerrard returned to action playing for Liverpool reserves against Wolves following a lengthy lay-off through injury in November, 2004. A larger than usual attendance was expected at Telford for the game but no-one envisaged the gates having to be shut with 6,280 supporters – the majority of them having travelled down from Merseyside – packed inside the ground. The attendance was a record for the non-League club since their ground had been redeveloped. Liverpool won the game with a late goal from Neil Mellor whilst Gerrard successfully made his return, coming on at the start of the second half and playing for the 45 minutes. Just five days earlier the stadium had housed a reserve game between Wolves and Everton that attracted just 359 supporters.

NO REPRIEVE

A blizzard forced the referee to abandon the Black Country derby at the interval in December 1962, with Wolves two goals to the good against West Bromwich Albion. Chris Crowe and Alan Hinton were the men whose strikes were wiped from the record books. Any Baggies fans thinking their team had got a reprieve were proved to be mistaken when the game was restaged the following March. Although Crowe didn't get onto the scoresheet, Terry Wharton registered a hat-trick and Hinton and Barry Stobart netted two each in what was a 7-0 rout.

BROTHERS IN ARMS

When Wolves and Newcastle United met in a First Division clash at Molineux in February, 1973, Kenny Hibbitt opened the scoring with a 22nd-minute volley to delight the home crowd. A Hibbitt also got the game's other goal – Newcastle's 56th-minute equaliser. It was a deflected effort and the scorer wasn't Kenny, but his brother Terry who was playing for the Tynesiders. Then, in February 2006, Leon Cort scored an equalising goal for Hull City against Wolves on Humberside but big brother Carl had the last laugh by grabbing a last-minute goal to give visitors Wanderers a 3-2 win.

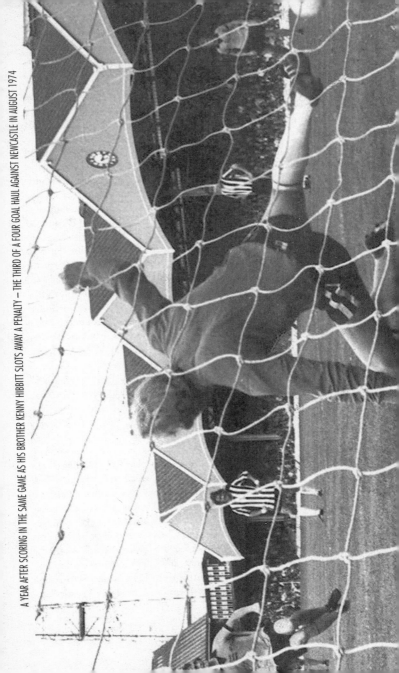

A YEAR AFTER SCORING IN THE SAME GAME AS HIS BROTHER KENNY HIBBITT SLOTS AWAY A PENALTY – THE THIRD OF A FOUR GOAL HAUL AGAINST NEWCASTLE IN AUGUST 1974

CHARITY SHIELD 1958

Wolves fielded an inexperienced trio in their front line for the 1958 Charity Shield against Bolton at Burnden Park. Gerry Mannion was making his first team debut, Cliff Durandt was playing in only his second senior game whilst Des Horne had played just one more. Joe Dean – who began in the Bolton goal – was on for only 14 minutes before he dislocated a shoulder and was eventually replaced by regular goalkeeper Eddie Hopkinson after a 10-minute stand-in by Nat Lofthouse. Because he had been chosen to play for the Football League the next day, Hopkinson was originally not allowed to take part but two Football League selectors agreed, because of the emergency, to his playing and he left his seat in the stand to take over from Lofthouse. After Jimmy Murray had hit the post and Mannion had missed a sitter, Wolves were made to pay for not making the most of their territorial supremacy when Fred Hill and Neville Bannister scored shortly before the break. Bolton had things pretty much their own way after the restart with Lofthouse hitting two (in the 57th and 67th minutes) before Durandt netted a last-minute consolation to make the final score 4-1 in the Trotters' favour. Wolves: Finlayson; Stuart, Harris; Flowers, Wright, Clamp; Mannion, Durandt, Murray, Mason, Horne.

SENT TO COVENTRY: IN IRELAND

The freezing conditions of the winter of 1963 forced many postponements in England. Between December 15 and March 9, Wolves were able to play in only four games – just one of them being at Molineux. So club officials arranged to play two friendly games with Coventry City in Ireland, the first of which took place in Cork on February 9. The weather in the Irish city was much milder than in England but the Cork pitch was in an extremely heavy condition. Three goals in a 13-minute second-half spell won the game for Wolves with Ron Flowers, Barry Stobart and Chris Crowe the scorers against the Third Division side in front of a 7,000 crowd. Eleven days later the teams met again, this time in Belfast, and 5,000 watched Wolves run out as 6-3 victors. Terry Wharton, Crowe, Ted Farmer, Stobart and Alan Hinton – with a brace – were the men on target for Wanderers.

BROKEN STICKS

One of the bigger shocks in the colourful history of the FA Cup came in 1957 when Bournemouth – of the Third Division (South) – came to Wolverhampton and beat one of the country's top teams. Winger Reg Cutler made a double mark on the game. Not only did he hit the only goal of the cup tie, but he also brought the goal frame crashing down at the South Bank end of Molineux when he ran into a post. Play was only able to resume after lengthy first aid to the woodwork. It was at the opposite end of the ground that a similar incident occurred on the opening day of the 1973/74 campaign. Derek Dougan had put Wolves one up against Norwich City and when he lobbed a second midway through the second-half, Canaries goalkeeper Kevin Keelan fell into the back of the net in his attempts to keep the ball out. He succeeded only in bringing the goal down upon himself. Keelan was stretchered off whilst a 16-minute break was needed to repair the damage. He was able to resume after the restart but couldn't prevent his team from going down 3-1.

REPLAY MASSACRE

A first round FA Cup tie between Watford and Wolves at Cassio Road in January 1912, finished goalless. But the replay against the Southern League side, at Molineux, proved to be an entirely different affair. Billy Halligan led the way with a hat-trick, Jack Needham and Sammy Brooks weighed in with two each, and Billy Harrison, George Hedley and Bob Young all got one as Wolves registered a 10-0 triumph over the Hornets.

EVERYONE'S HAPPY

When Wolves and Sheffield United met at the end of the 1988/89 season, both sides were looking for a point from the game. A draw would result in Wolves finishing as Third Division Champions and the Blades would end the campaign as runners-up to join the Molineux men in the second tier of English football. The result was a 2-2 draw and so both sets of players and supporters went home happy.

BILLY

In these days of over-hyped superlatives, there is little doubt that Billy Wright would have been fêted as a superstar both on and off the pitch. But the man who captained England and, through their glory days, Wolverhampton Wanderers, was a modest and unassuming character – a real gentleman. Not for him were the fast cars and the high life – the captain of club and country quite happily made his way home to his digs in Claregate on the local bus service. William Ambrose Wright was born in Ironbridge, Shropshire, on February 6, 1924. He attended Madeley Senior School and was a star for the school team although not as a defender, but as a centre-forward. In one game he netted 10 goals. He was an Arsenal supporter as a lad but when Wolves advertised in the local newspaper for youngsters to go to Molineux for trials, Billy was one of the first to apply. He was only 14 years old when he made his debut for Wolves in a B team game against Walsall Wood in the Walsall Minor League after being accepted on an eight-month trial. Major Frank Buckley, Wolves manager, wasn't convinced of the youngster's talents and at first he told Billy that he wasn't going to make it as a professional footballer. Luckily for Wolves he had a change of heart and Billy Wright went on to become one of the greatest names in not only the long and illustrious history of Wolverhampton Wanderers, but world soccer too. Billy made his debut for the first team shortly after the outbreak of the war in the 2-1 victory at Notts County. At 17, he signed as a professional and he turned out as a guest for Leicester City along with Jimmy Mullen after the worsening war situation prompted Wolves to suspend competitive football. For the Foxes, he played as both a forward and a defender before he returned to Molineux in 1942, and broke his ankle in a cup-tie with West Bromwich Albion. He joined the army in 1943 as a Physical Training Instructor and he played for Wolves whenever possible – making over 100 appearances for the club in wartime football. When peace was restored and soccer returned to normality, Billy was to miss only eight games playing in the wing half position of that first post-war season in 1946/7. Stan Cullis retired from the playing side of the game at the end of that campaign and Billy was appointed captain of the club in his place. In the following two

seasons he was to miss only 10 games and he picked up his first major honour when Wolves overcame Leicester City in the 1949 FA Cup final. In 1954, Wolves did what they had been threatening to do ever since the seasons that led up to the war. After so many near things they finally captured the League Championship. Billy Wright's captaincy was an inspiration to the team who then set about some of Europe's finest clubs and demolished them in those never-to-be-forgotten floodlit friendlies. The next three years were again to prove almost, but not quite, as the team finished second, third and sixth respectively before in 1957/58 and 1958/59 the Championship trophy was again held aloft by Billy. In nine seasons in the 1950s he only missed 31 games for Wolves and several of those absences were caused by international call-ups. Billy's record for England was exceptional. He was capped on 105 occasions, 90 of which saw him skippering the national side. He played his first full international against Northern Ireland in 1946, and by the time he made his last appearance 12 years later in the 8-1 thrashing of the United States in Los Angeles, he had missed only three games for his country. Of his 105 games, 60 were won, 23 drawn, 21 lost and one game was abandoned. The first player in the world to reach 100 international appearances, his record of 105 caps was to stand for 11 years until it was broken by Bobby Charlton in 1970. Billy Wright, captain of Wolves and England, was one of the game's greatest ambassadors. He played his last League game for Wolves in the penultimate match of 1958/59 when Wolves overcame Leicester 3-0 at Molineux. Shortly afterwards he was awarded the CBE for his services to football and he announced his retirement from the game just before the start of the next season. He bade Molineux and its grateful fans farewell in the annual pre-season Colours v Whites practice game. A year earlier he had grabbed the headlines of the national press for non-footballing reasons when he married Joy Beverley of the popular singing trio, The Beverley Sisters. Billy became manager of his boyhood heroes, Arsenal, in 1962 and four years later he left Highbury and was thereafter associated with sports coverage on ATV (later Central). He retired in 1989, and, in May 1990, he delighted Wolves fans both young and old when he returned to Molineux as a director for one of the most popular homecomings of all time. It was with typical modesty that he accepted the honour of having the new Waterloo Road Stand named after him in 1993. Just over a year later, in September 1994 at the age of 70, Billy Wright passed away after a fight against cancer. His funeral the following week brought the centre of Wolverhampton to a standstill as the town said farewell to its favourite footballing son. On the second anniversary of his death, a magnificent statue of the legend was unveiled outside the main entrance of Molineux.

JIMMY WAS FIRST

One-club man Jimmy Mullen won 12 full caps playing for England. But when the winger played his fourth game of the 12, he wrote himself into the history books. The match took place against Belgium in Brussels in May 1950 just prior to England's departure to Brazil for the World Cup Finals. Against Belgium, when Jimmy was sent on as a replacement for Newcastle's Jackie Milburn, he became the first-ever England substitute. And he celebrated his introduction with one of England's goals in a 4-1 victory. In the World Cup he played in the 2-0 win over Chile and the shock defeat at the hands of the United States of America. Jimmy played his last international in the 1954 World Cup Finals against the hosts Switzerland. He scored in a 2-0 triumph – his sixth goal for England – giving him a strike rate of one every two games for his country.

FIRST TROPHY

The imposing Wrekin Cup was the first silverware won by Wolves just seven years after the formation of the club. They beat Hadley (Shropshire) in the 1884 Final played at Eyton Park, Wellington, on May 31, by an impressive 11-0. The winning team was: I. Griffiths, Cliff, Mason, Davidson, Baynton, Blackham, Pearson, Lowder, Brodie, Hadley, J. Griffiths. Jack Brodie scored six of the goals and Arthur Lowder three. En route to the final Wolves had beaten St Paul's (Lozells) 7-0, arch rivals in the town, Stafford Road, by 3-0 and, in the semi-final, Shrewsbury Castle Blues by 5-0 in a replayed game – the original fixture being declared void because of a discrepancy after Wolves had won 2-0.

CHARITY SHIELD 1959

The 1959 Charity Shield was played, for the first time, as a curtain-raiser to the new season. In later years that would not only become the norm but the game would be switched to Wembley to increase its prestige even more. For the first time since his official appointment as club skipper in succession to Billy Wright, Eddie Stuart led out Wolves. Forest took the lead on 37 minutes against the run of play. Norman Deeley, in his own penalty area, miskicked when he tried to hook the ball clear and Tommy Wilson back-headed the ball past Malcolm Finlayson. Wolves levelled within a minute after a foul by Jim Iley on Peter Broadbent, who took the free-kick and slipped the ball to man-of-the-match Ron Flowers whose cross was met with a running header by Jimmy Murray to make it 1-1. Broadbent put Wolves in front on 56 minutes when he headed in Micky Lill's lobbed centre and Lill hit the third nine minutes from time when he took advantage of hesitancy between centre-half Bobby McKinlay and keeper Chick Thomson. Wolves had Welshman Gwyn Jones deputising for Gerry Harris who had been injured in the public practice game a week earlier. It was the first and so far only time Wolves had won the Shield outright. Wolves: Finlayson, Stuart, Jones, Clamp, Showell, Flowers, Lill, Mason, Murray, Broadbent, Deeley.

FALLOWFIELD FIRST AND LAST

When Wolves beat Everton at Fallowfield in the 1893 FA Cup, it was the first time the Final had taken place outside London. It was also the only time that the venue was used for the Final.

THE 'I'S HAVE IT

Up to the start of the 21st century Wolves had only ever fielded two players whose name began with the letter I – Bob Iverson, and Ted Ivill, who played for the club in the 1930s. Then three came along in one season 2002/03 – Paul Ince, Denis Irwin and Ivar Ingimarsson. Since then, goalkeeper Carl Ikeme has made his debut in the first team and joined the list.

REDS REVENGE

When Wolves beat Liverpool by 5-1 at Anfield in December 1946, they leapfrogged the Merseyside club to go top of the table. But the Reds were to get their revenge at the end of a campaign prolonged because of the severe winter of 1947. The return, at Molineux, took place on May 31 and Wolves went into the game knowing that a win and the two points would give them a first ever League Championship. Six of the Liverpool side and nine of the Wolves team had played in the first game but one of the Molineux absentees was the prolific Dennis Westcott who had struck four at Anfield and was the club's leading scorer with 38 League goals. Westcott had hurt his knee in the home game against Blackburn Rovers two weeks earlier and his loss to the side was a huge one. Liverpool were two up at the interval through Jack Balmer – who opened the scoring on 20 minutes – and Albert Stubbins who ran from the half-way line before beating Bert Williams eight minutes before the break. A Jimmy Dunn lob, midway through the second period, put Wolves back in contention but the visitors held on to go top of the table – a point above the despondent Wanderers team. Manchester United took the runners-up spot on goal average and Liverpool were confirmed as champions two weeks after their game with Wolves when Stoke City also blew their chances of a first title when they lost 2-1 at Sheffield United.

THREE TIMES CHAMPIONS

Wolves made it a third League Championship in the decade of the 1950s when they captured the title in 1959. As reigning champions the side made a promising start with Bobby Mason's treble helping cement a 5-1 win over Nottingham Forest. But two trips to London in a five-day spell offered little but concern with a 2-0 reversal at West Ham being followed by a 6-2 trouncing at Chelsea. When West Ham provided the next opposition at Molineux, the game finished all square at one-all in front of a 52,317 crowd. Then a four-game winning run which included a double over Aston Villa propelled the team up into second place on goal average behind Luton Town. Thirteen victories and seven defeats came in the next

21 games with Portsmouth on the wrong end of a Christmas double that saw Wanderers win 5-3 at Fratton Park on Boxing Day and 7-0 at Molineux 24 hours later. The 2-1 setback against Manchester United at Old Trafford on February 21 proved to be the final defeat of the League campaign although that weekend it was costly as Arsenal leapfrogged above Stan Cullis' men to lead the division by a point. But the remaining games saw Wolves drop just three points from a possible 26 and they finished the campaign a comfortable six points in front of runners-up Manchester United. A total of 22 players were called upon by Cullis. Jimmy Murray was the leading scorer with 21 goals closely followed by Peter Broadbent who netted one fewer. Broadbent did, however, finish as overall leading scorer as he scored two in the European Cup tie with Schalke 04.

FOOTBALL LEAGUE DIVISION ONE

		Pl	W	D	L	F	A	W	D	L	F	A	Pts
1	WOLVES	42	15	3	3	68	19	13	2	6	42	30	61
2	Manchester United	42	14	4	3	58	27	10	3	8	45	39	55
3	Arsenal	42	14	3	4	53	29	7	5	9	35	39	50
4	Bolton Wanderers	42	14	3	4	56	30	6	7	8	23	36	50
5	West Brom Albion	42	8	7	6	41	33	10	6	5	47	35	49
6	West Ham United	42	15	3	3	59	29	6	3	12	26	41	48
7	Burnley	42	11	4	6	41	29	8	6	7	40	41	48
8	Blackpool	42	12	7	2	39	13	6	4	11	27	36	47
9	Birmingham City	42	14	1	6	54	35	6	5	10	30	33	46
10	Blackburn Rovers	42	12	3	6	48	28	5	7	9	28	42	44
11	Newcastle United	42	11	3	7	40	29	6	4	11	40	51	41
12	Preston North End	42	9	3	9	40	39	8	4	9	30	38	41
13	Nottingham Forest	42	9	4	8	37	32	8	2	11	34	42	40
14	Chelsea	42	13	2	6	52	37	5	2	14	25	61	40
15	Leeds United	42	8	7	6	28	27	7	2	12	29	47	39
16	Everton	42	11	3	7	39	38	6	1	14	32	49	38
17	Luton Town	42	11	6	4	50	26	1	7	13	18	45	37
18	Tottenham Hotspur	42	10	3	8	56	42	3	7	11	29	53	36
19	Leicester City	42	7	6	8	34	36	4	4	13	33	62	32
20	Manchester City	42	8	7	6	40	32	3	2	16	24	63	31
21	Aston Villa	42	8	5	8	31	33	3	3	15	27	54	30
22	Portsmouth	42	5	4	12	38	47	1	5	15	26	65	21

SMALL IN STATURE, BIG IN HEART

When Norman Deeley made his debut for the England Schoolboy team in a match against Wales at Coventry City's Highfield Road in 1948, he created an unusual record – that of being the shortest boy ever to play for the national team. Norman stood at just 4ft 4ins tall, seven inches smaller than the previous 'record holder' Raich Carter. By the time he made his first team debut for Wolves in August 1951, Norman had grown to five feet four and three quarters – less than an inch taller than his fellow right winger Johnny Hancocks who had made his last of his 378 appearances for the club in 1956. Johnny scored 168 goals for Wolves and he won three caps playing for England, a total restricted by his fear of flying and the presence of two of the game's greatest ever wingers, Stanley Matthews and Tom Finney. Norman also played for his country – winning two caps in 1959. At club level he won two Championship medals and he scored two of Wolves' three goals in the 1960 FA Cup Final triumph over Blackburn Rovers. He played 237 first team games for Stan Cullis and scored 75 goals.

COSTLY COMEBACK

Alun Evans became the first £100,000 teenager in Britain when he moved from Molineux to Liverpool in September 1968. A product of the club's youth system, Evans made a sensational start to what was a brief first-team career at Molineux. In his second game, in September 1967, he grabbed a last-minute winner in a 3-2 home win over Burnley prompting a headline from the local *Sporting Star* newspaper of 'Good Evans'. A week later he did it again with a last-minute equaliser at Sheffield Wednesday and this time the headline read 'Good Evans Again'. He scored just two more goals that season giving him a total of four from 20 games. The following term he made one more outing for Wanderers before his switch to Anfield. A fortnight after the transfer, exactly a year on from making his debut, he returned to Wolverhampton and scored two of Liverpool's six unanswered goals on what was a miserable afternoon for the home fans in the near-40,000 crowd.

LITTLE KNOWN RULE

Has any player won an international cap with as obscure a qualification as Paul Butler, who was Wolves' centre-half in their successful play-off triumph of 2003? As a Sunderland player he won his one and only cap for the Republic of Ireland thanks to the little known rule that his wife, Caroline, was Irish-born. Butler, born in Manchester, could have chosen any one of three countries to play for – his father's family were English and his mother's Welsh. Both Bobby Gould, who was then manager of Wales, and Mick McCarthy, Ireland's manager, approached Butler and he opted for the Irish. His cap came in the 3-2 friendly win over the Czech Republic at Lansdowne Road, Dublin, in February, 2000. Injury ruled Butler out of the internationals which followed and, by the time he had recovered, he had fallen down the pecking order of Irish central defenders.

NINE AT NINIAN

Wolves hold the joint record for an away win in the top-flight thanks to a 9-1 trouncing of Cardiff City at Ninian Park in September 1955. It was a particularly memorable game for Jimmy Mullen who scored one of the goals and had a hand in each of the other eight. Less than a minute had gone when Johnny Hancocks had the easiest of tasks to convert after Mullen's shot had struck the bar. After 10 minutes it was Hancocks again, this time scoring from 12 yards after taking a Mullen pass. Three minutes later Mullen got in on the act himself with the third before supplying the cross for Roy Swinbourne to score the fourth with just 20 minutes gone. Hancocks completed his hat-trick after yet another Mullen centre in the 34th minute and Swinbourne back-heeled the sixth after Mullen had helped on a Hancocks corner on 54 minutes. Peter Broadbent helped himself to two goals in the 66th and 75th minutes – the first after a Mullen corner and the other after a pass from the winger. The rout was completed by Swinbourne who made sure of his hat-trick by deflecting in Mullen's cross-shot nine minutes from time. Ron Stockin – who had moved from Molineux to Ninian Park in the previous year – then scored a consolation goal for the Bluebirds.

ON RECORD

Generally speaking, footballers are not noted for their musical recording works. Once purchased, footballing discs are usually played once and then consigned to the back of the record rack rarely to see the light of day again. There have been three vinyl offerings from Molineux personnel – an LP and two singles. The long player was issued in 1967 to celebrate the promotion back to Division One. It contained interviews and songs from the players including such classics as 'Oh, oh, oh oh what a luv'ly game' and 'The Hungry Wolves'. The record was entitled 'Wolves – Players At Ease'. When the team reached the 1980 League Cup Final a single called 'Wonderful Wolves' was released and to commemorate winning the Fourth Division Championship and reaching the Sherpa Van Trophy Final in 1988, the aptly titled 'We're Back' was issued. Records featuring two footballing brothers were also issued. 'Nice one Cyril' was released by the Cockney Chorus, Cyril being the late Spurs defender Cyril Knowles – whilst Billy Bragg penned 'God's Footballer' about brother Peter who quit soccer to become a Jehovah's Witness.

NON-LEAGUE OPPONENTS

Wolves have encountered 27 non-League opponents in FA Cup ties. Most of the games came prior to the First World War before the formation of the Third Divisions (North and South). Opponents in those days included Southampton, Crystal Palace, West Ham, Watford, Lincoln and Cardiff. Since the formation of the extra two divisions, Wolves have played six FA Cup ties against non-League teams – although four of the six are now current League members. In 1927, there was a 2-0 win against Carlisle United whilst two years later Mansfield enjoyed a shock 1-0 win at Molineux. In 1946, Welsh works team Lovells Athletic were beaten by a 12-3 aggregate over two legs, and Altrincham lost 5-0 in a third round game in 1966. Probably the lowest point in Wolves' history came in November 1986, when, after two drawn games, Chorley grabbed the headlines with a 3-0 victory at Burnden Park. Just a year later, with fortunes beginning to improve, Cheltenham Town lost 5-1 at Molineux in a first round tie.

ON THE ROOF AND ON RECORD: THE WOLVES SIDE OF 1988

SCORING DEBUT AGAINST FUTURE CLUB

Ronnie Allen could have had no idea that the opponents in his debut game for West Bromwich Albion would be guided to promotion under his management 17 years later. A crowd of 60,945 – then a League record at The Hawthorns – witnessed his first game as Wolves and the Baggies fought out a one-all draw. Johnny Hancocks had fired Wolves into the lead but his strike was cancelled out as Allen marked his big day with the equaliser. He arrived at Molineux, initially as coach, in March 1965 and took over from Andy Beattie in the role of acting manager the following September. In the summer of 1966, the 'acting' part of his job description was dropped as he took the role on a full-time basis. At the end of the season that followed, Wolves were promoted back to the top-flight. Three of Ronnie's signings – Derek Dougan, Mike Bailey and Derek Parkin – were to play leading roles in the club's long-term future. He was replaced by Bill McGarry in November 1968 after a mediocre start to the campaign had left Wolves in the bottom half of the table.

ABANDONED

Wolves have suffered just two abandoned games since the Second World War. In January 1961, fog meant that the First Division game at Bloomfield Road, Blackpool, was halted after just seven minutes when the score was 0-0. On Boxing Day 1962, Wolves were 2-0 up against West Bromwich at Molineux when a blizzard forced an end to proceedings during the interval break. Back in November 1893, Everton were 2-0 up at Molineux when the game was abandoned through snow, and, in December of the following year, a game at Stoke was called off after just four minutes also because of snow. In March 1903, Liverpool were two up after 50 minutes play at Anfield when heavy rain forced the referee to send the teams from the waterlogged pitch. Shortly before Christmas 1936, just seven minutes of Wolves' game against Leeds were left when a blizzard ended the game. Wolves were a goal to the good at the time although they were without the services of goalkeeper Alex Scott – who had been sent off – and Stan Cullis, who had sustained an injury.

ALL MY OWN WORK

In 1960 Stan Cullis' book 'All For Wolves' was released. It was a sporting book with a difference for the manager of Wolves didn't use a ghostwriter to put his words to paper. Apart from the foreword by Billy Wright, Stan wrote every one of the 226 pages himself. It was something he was, quite correctly, intensely proud of.

FIRST CUP SUBSTITUTES

Les Wilson was the first substitute used by Wolves in an FA Cup fixture – the Canadian replacing Ernie Hunt in a fourth round replay against Oldham Athletic at Molineux in February 1967. In the League Cup the honour fell to Paul Walker in a fourth round tie at Queens Park Rangers in October 1969, when he went on in place of Dave Wagstaffe. Walker was also the club's first substitute in European competition at the end of that 1969/70 season when he replaced Mike Bailey in a home Anglo Italian Cup tie against Fiorentina.

SHORT TIME

Wellington-born Ian Wallace's League career lasted for all of three minutes and it has to be the shortest in Wolves' history. He came on for Ernie Hunt just before the end of a 4-0 victory over Blackburn Rovers in a Second Division fixture in September, 1966. Steve Blackwell faired little better in his solitary outing for Wolves. He played for the final 18 minutes of a Second Division game at Wimbledon's Plough Lane in April 1985 after he replaced Tony Evans. Mike Kent did have the satisfaction of playing twice in the top-flight for Wolves. He played for all but the first 13 minutes of a home defeat at the hands of Sunderland in March 1970 – as a replacement for Dave Wagstaffe. But he then had to wait for another two years, virtually to the day, before he got another chance. This time it came at The Dell as Wolves beat Southampton 2-1. But there was just three minutes of the game remaining when Kent replaced Bernard Shaw. His next League action was with Gillingham for whom he made 11 appearances and then he had four outings in a brief spell with Sheffield Wednesday.

CHARITY SHIELD 1960

When John Connelly netted for Burnley just four minutes from time, it looked as if the winger had won the 1960 Charity Shield for the Lancashire club. But Jimmy Murray popped up with an equalising goal two minutes later to ensure that Wolves shared the trophy for the third time from the five that they had competed for it. The visitors didn't have the best of preparation for the game with their train from Manchester to Burnley being delayed meaning they arrived at the ground only 20 minutes before kick-off. Brian Miller gave the Clarets a 10th-minute lead which was cancelled out by Norman Deeley's scrambled effort nine minutes after the break. Then came the dramatic finale. Wolves: Sidebottom, Showell, Harris, Kirkham, Stuart, Clamp, Mannion, Stobart, Murray, Broadbent, Deeley.

FOUR CENTURIES

Wolves are the only club to have scored over 100 League goals in four successive seasons. They scored 103 in 1957/58, 110 (1958/59), 106 (1959/60) and 103 in 1960/61.

BACK AT THE SECOND ATTEMPT

After the disastrous 1964/65 season had seen the parting of the ways for the club and Stan Cullis – and had ended in relegation – Wolves were tipped for an instant return to the First Division. But they had to be satisfied with sixth place, five points shy of a promotion spot in their first attempt to return to the top flight. The following term didn't start too brightly either, with defeats suffered at the hands of Birmingham City and Ipswich Town before a nine-game unbeaten run lifted the side to the top of the table. Apart from a bleak pre-Christmas spell of three reversals in four games, the form was pretty consistent and, from mid-January until the third week of April, a run of 11 wins and three draws from 14 games put Wanderers in pole position for the Second Division title. But Coventry City had kept pace and when the sides met at Highfield Road three games from the end of the campaign, a record 51,455 crowd saw the Sky Blues put themselves in contention for the top spot with a 3-1 win. But Wolves' destiny was still in their own hands. After a comfortable 4-1 home victory over Norwich City, Ronnie Allen's men needed a point from their trip to Crystal Palace to be crowned as champions. But the team had an 'off day' at Selhurst Park and slumped to a 4-1 defeat – the heaviest setback of the season, with Coventry taking advantage and the honours by beating Millwall 3-1 at Highfield Road. Dave Wagstaffe was the only ever-present and he also took part in all six of the cup games that season, while Mike Bailey's muscle injury cost the side his expertise as captain in the final game at Palace otherwise he would have joined Wagstaffe with a 100 per cent appearance record. Ernie Hunt top-scored with 21 League and Cup goals.

FOOTBALL LEAGUE DIVISION TWO

		Pl	W	D	L	F	A	W	D	L	F	A	Pts
1	Coventry City	42	17	3	1	46	16	6	10	5	28	27	59
2	WOLVES	42	15	4	2	53	20	10	4	7	35	28	58
3	Carlisle United	42	15	3	3	42	16	8	3	10	29	38	52
4	Blackburn Rovers	42	13	6	2	33	11	6	7	8	23	35	51
5	Ipswich Town	42	11	8	2	45	25	6	8	7	25	29	50
6	Huddersfield Town	42	14	3	4	36	17	6	6	9	22	29	49
7	Crystal Palace	42	14	4	3	42	23	5	6	10	19	32	48
8	Millwall	42	14	5	2	33	17	4	4	13	16	41	45
9	Bolton Wanderers	42	10	7	4	36	19	4	7	10	28	39	42
10	Birmingham City	42	11	5	5	42	23	5	3	13	28	43	40
11	Norwich City	42	10	7	4	31	21	3	7	11	18	34	40
12	Hull City	42	11	5	5	46	25	5	2	14	31	47	39
13	Preston North End	42	14	3	4	44	23	2	4	15	21	44	39
14	Portsmouth	42	7	5	9	34	37	6	8	7	25	33	39
15	Bristol City	42	10	8	3	38	22	2	6	13	18	40	38
16	Plymouth Argyle	42	12	4	5	42	21	2	5	14	17	37	37
17	Derby County	42	8	6	7	40	32	4	6	11	28	40	36
18	Rotherham United	42	10	5	6	39	28	3	5	13	22	42	36
19	Charlton Athletic	42	11	4	6	34	16	2	5	14	15	37	35
20	Cardiff City	42	9	7	5	43	28	3	2	16	18	59	33
21	Northampton Town	42	8	6	7	28	33	4	0	17	19	51	30
22	Bury	42	9	3	9	31	30	2	3	16	18	53	28

WHAT A START FOR WILLIE

Willie Carr couldn't in his wildest dreams have hoped for a better debut after his switch from Coventry City to Wolves in March 1975. His first game in gold and black was against Chelsea at Molineux and, after John Richards had fired Wolves into a 23rd-minute lead, Willie got in on the act with Wolves' second just two minutes later. Although the Londoners pulled a goal back, further strikes from Kenny Hibbitt, Mike Bailey, Steve Kindon, Dave Wagstaffe plus another effort from Richards made the final tally 7-1 in favour of Wanderers.

NEVER A CROSS WORD!

Stan Cullis was a manager both feared and respected by his players. But the man who served Wolves with such distinction as both player and manager never used bad language. An example of his use of words to good effect without the need to swear came at the interval of a game when he was berating the efforts of his team. A squad member, not involved in the game, was sat in the dressing-room grinning at the roasting his team-mates were getting when he was spotted by the manager who is reputed to have said: "Son, if you're a reserve to this lot, then you have nothing to smile about."

EUROPEAN DOUBLE

Derek Dougan and John McAlle share the honour of playing most European competition games for Wolves. Each turned out 18 times in UEFA Cup ties. Dougan also holds the scoring record of 12 goals from those 18 games.

TOP OF EACH TREE

When Wolves won the League title in 1954, they became the first club in England to win each of the three divisions (until 1958 the Third Division was divided into two sections – North and South). And the club became the first to finish top of all four sections when they won the Fourth Division Championship in 1988 before adding the Third Division title 12 months later.

TREBLE WITH A DIFFERENCE

There was an unusual threesome when Wolves beat Portsmouth 3-2 in a third round FA Cup replay in January 1965. It was an afternoon when the three home goals were scored by a player wearing the number nine shirt. Nothing very strange in that but there was no hat-trick that day as Ray Crawford began the game wearing number 10 only to emerge for the second half sporting a number nine shirt. As centre-forward Hughie McIlmoyle had not changed his top, the team played the whole of the second half with two number nines on the pitch. McIlmoyle had scored twice in the first half and Crawford hit the third goal after the break to complete a treble with a difference.

DOUBLING UP INITIALLY

Wolverhampton Wanderers are one of just five clubs in the English Leagues to have the same letter at the start of both of their titled names. The others are Coventry City, Cardiff City, Wycombe Wanderers and Chester City. A Wolves team comprising players with the same initial for their Christian name and surname could be: Matt Murray, George Garratly, Steve Stoutt, George Getgood, William Wright, Campbell Chapman, Harry Hooper, Chris Crowe, Derek Dougan, Sammy Smyth, Michael McIndoe. Others include: Alan Ainscow, Phil Parkes, Mick Matthews, Billy Beats, Brian Birch, Cavan Chapman, Jackery Jones, Jack Jones, Robert Rosario and Colin Cameron.

MEMORABLE BUS RIDE

Billy Wright was in the last stages of a return journey from Copenhagen, where he had played for England in a goalless draw against the Danes in September 1948, when he received the news that he had been made captain of his country from a most unlikely source. He was travelling on the bus from Wolverhampton to his digs in Claregate when the conductress informed him that he had been made skipper for the forthcoming international against Northern Ireland in Belfast. The clippie offered Billy the local evening newspaper to confirm the news.

TOO CLOSE FOR COMFORT

As the 1961/62 season was drawing to a close, Wolves, who were struggling in the lower reaches of the First Division, travelled to London to take on bottom placed Chelsea at Stamford Bridge. Terry Wharton gave the visitors an 8th-minute lead – and further goals from John Kirkham, Peter McParland and a pair from Chris Crowe against a Bobby Tambling penalty meant that Wolves were 5-1 up with just six minutes to play. But Barry Bridges, Peter Brabrook and Bert Murray all scored for Chelsea in a five-minute spell leaving Wanderers to desperately cling on for the final minute and added time to be sure of the two points they were seemingly cruising towards just a few moments earlier. There was another comeback in the corresponding fixture during the previous season with Chelsea this time having the upper hand thanks to a Jimmy Greaves hat-trick. The Pensioners were 3-1 up, with Des Horne having scored for Wolves, with just 16 minutes to go. But a brace from Jimmy Murray, who scored in the 74th and 83rd minutes, gave Wolves a point from their journey south.

STEVE STUNS ANFIELD

Steve Mardenborough's only goal for Wolves, in the event, did not alter the course of a turbulent 1983/84 season for the club. With the campaign having just passed its halfway stage, and with Wolves rooted firmly at the bottom of the table, a trip to Anfield wasn't the best of prospects given the circumstances – especially as Liverpool were the reigning League Champions and were once again nicely placed at the top. But the form book was to be turned upside down on that January day as Wolves beat the Reds on their own ground for the first time in 33 years. Mardenborough didn't even know he was playing until the Saturday morning when Mel Eves was declared unfit but the young striker made the most of his opportunity by scoring the game's only goal in the ninth minute when he rose to head a Danny Crainie cross beyond the dive of Bruce Grobbelaar – although the ball looked to go in off his shoulder as it looped past the keeper. Mardenborough was to make just 11 appearances for Wolves before he moved to Swansea City in the summer of 1984 – this after a loan spell with Cambridge United.

WHAT A START

A pre-season friendly at Worcester in 1995 had an amazing opening. From the kick-off City's Steve Ferguson touched the ball to team-mate Phil Mason who had spotted Wolves keeper Andy de Bont off his line. Mason launched a terrific shot from the halfway line that sailed over De Bont into the net. The goal was unofficially timed at five seconds. Worcester added another to go two up before Brian Law, Dominic Foley and Paul Emblen (younger brother of Wolves midfielder Neil, who was on trial) all scored to turn the game around and win it for Wolves.

TRAGIC

Two players who met tragic ends in the prime of their lives were David Wykes and goalkeeper Jimmy Utterson. Wykes made the last of his 179 appearances for Wolves against Stoke City in October 1895. Just a day later he died in hospital suffering from pneumonia and typhoid fever. A right-winger, he scored 69 goals for the club. Utterson was making his 14th appearance for Wanderers, at Middlesbrough in September 1935, when he was the victim of an accidental kick to the head. He never recovered from the injury and sadly passed away in hospital shortly before Christmas that year.

TEXACO SUCCESS

Wolves' first flirtation with a sponsored competition came in the 1970/71 campaign when they entered and won the Texaco Cup. And the triumph came despite failing to win in three of the four home games in the aggregate ties. After winning away at Dundee (2-1) in the first round, there followed a goalless draw at Molineux. A 3-0 win at Morton was followed by a 2-1 home reversal before Derry City of Northern Ireland succumbed to a 5-0 aggregate after they had gone down 1-0 at Brandywell Park. The first leg of the final, against Hearts, saw Wolves gain a 3-1 advantage thanks to a brace from Hugh Curran and a Mike Bailey strike, but the second leg was a tame affair that the Scots won 1-0 in front of a 28,000 crowd that had the consolation of watching Mike Bailey lift the trophy in the competition's inaugural season.

FA CUP FINAL 1960

The 1960 FA Cup certainly won't go down in the history books as one of the most attractive of finals. It was a mediocre affair that was goalless and virtually chanceless until the 41st minute when Blackburn Rovers' left-half Mick McGrath slid the ball into his own net as he attempted to clear Barry Stobart's low centre. Then, just before the break, the Lancastrians lost full-back Dave Whelan who suffered a broken leg which meant, in those pre-substitute days, that Rovers had to play the second period with just 10 men. They held out gamely until midway through the half when Norman Deeley skipped past two challenges and planted the ball into the net after taking a cross from Des Horne. Then, two minutes from time, Deeley completed the scoring when he turned and drove the ball into the roof of the net from close range after Stobart had set up the opportunity. Stobart, just 21 years old and with only five senior appearances behind him, was a headline-making replacement for Bobby Mason.

Round/scorers	Opponents/venue	Score
Round 3	Newcastle United (a)	2-2
Clamp, Flowers		
Replay	Newcastle United (h)	4-2
Flowers, Deeley, Murray, Horne		
Round 4	Charlton Athletic (h)	2-1
Broadbent, Horne		
Round 5	Luton Town (a)	4-1
Clamp, Mason 2, Murray		
Round 6	Leicester City (a)	2-1
Broadbent, Chalmers og		
Semi-Final	Aston Villa (the Hawthorns)	1-0
Deeley		
Final	Blackburn Rovers (Wembley)	3-0
Deeley 2, McGrath og		

Wolves 1960 FA Cup Final team: Finlayson, Showell, Harris, Clamp, Slater, Flowers, Deeley, Stobart, Murray, Broadbent, Horne.

DOUBLE GLORY FOR THE REVEREND

The year of 1908 was a more than memorable one for the Reverend Kenneth Gunnery Hunt. Not only did he win an FA Cup winners medal when Wolves beat Newcastle United at Crystal Palace, but he also took gold in the Olympic Games – which were held in London that year – when the United Kingdom beat Denmark by 2-0 in the soccer final at White City. Although he had a 14-year association with Wolves after making his debut in 1906, his studies at Trent College and Oxford University limited his appearances for the club to just 61.

QUICK FIRE DISMISSAL

On the opening day of the 2000/01 season, Sheffield Wednesday goalkeeper Kevin Pressman, claimed an unwelcome record when he was sent off after just 13 seconds of Wolves' game with the Owls at Molineux after he had handled Temuri Ketsbaia's goalbound shot outside his area. Although he was three seconds outside the world record set by Giuseppe Lorenzo of Bologna, in 1990, he became the fastest to be dismissed in England – beating the 19 seconds that Mark Smith of Crewe Alexandra lasted in 1994. Although Wednesday had to play for 89 minutes with 10 men, they still took a point from the game when Andy Booth headed home shortly before the end to cancel out Ketsbaia's first-half opener.

SPOILERS

Wolves was the unlikely team that put an end to Reading's record breaking opening to the 1985/86 Third Division campaign. The Berkshire side had won their first 13 League games and looked certain to stretch their record when they entertained a Molineux team that had won just twice from their opening 13 fixtures and that lay one off the bottom of the table. But a brace from midfielder Derek Ryan – who opened the scoring and then equalised after Kevin Bremner and Trevor Senior had given the home side the advantage – saw Wolves take a point and end Reading's run.

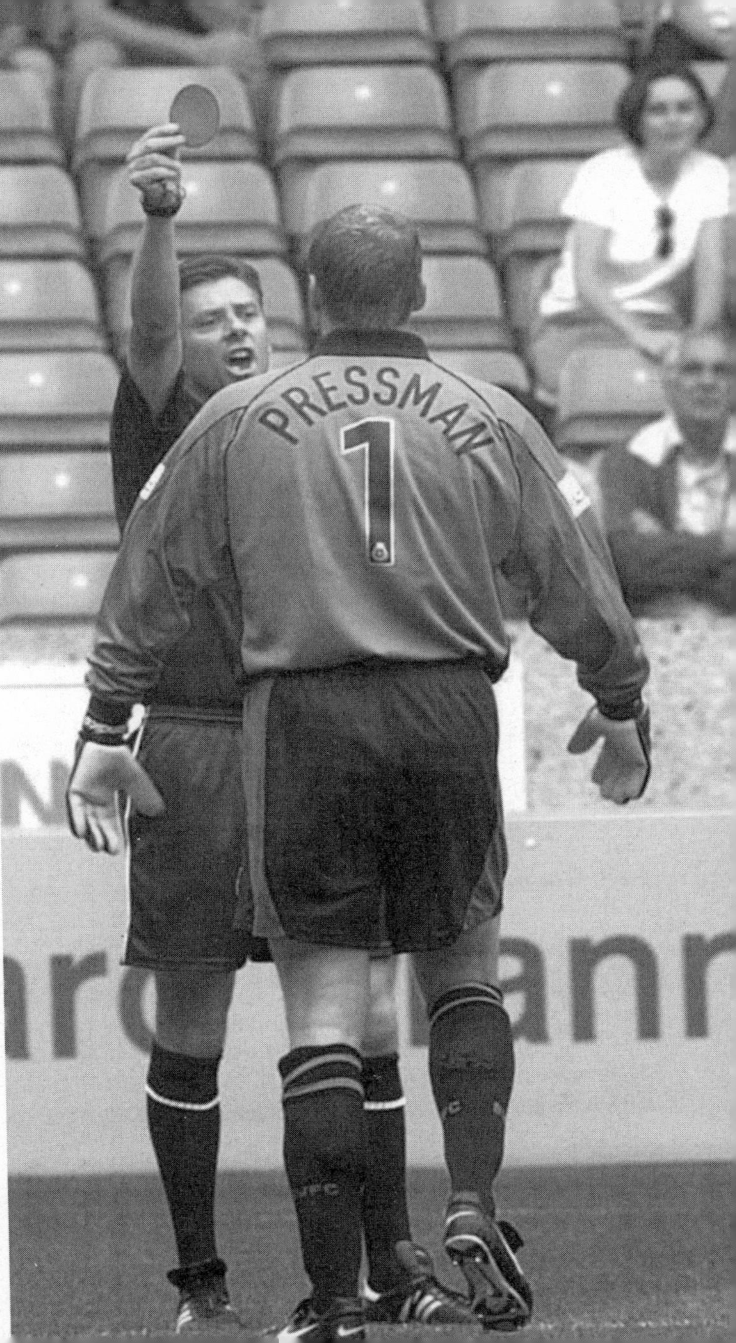

KEVIN PRESSMAN SEES RED AFTER JUST 13 SECONDS

HAPPY HUNTING GROUND

Maine Road was certainly a happy hunting ground for Wolves in an eight-year spell between 1955 and 1962. During that period Manchester City lost five and drew three of their games with Wolves on their own territory. Wolves rattled in 28 goals in the eight games – including six in a 6-4 win in September 1959.

SO CLOSE

Wolves were so close to UEFA Cup glory in 1972 after seeing off some of Europe's finest, only to succumb to Tottenham Hotspur in what was the first – and so far only – all English final. The first leg, played at Molineux, was refereed by Tofik Bakhramov who attained notoriety as a linesman by signalling that Geoff Hurst's shot had crossed the German goalline in the 1966 World Cup final. Wolves dominated a largely chanceless opening 45 minutes although Martin Chivers did hit the top of a post with an early free-kick. After the break, Wolves increased the pressure; forcing four corners in two minutes and seeing shots from John Richards and Kenny Hibbitt cleared off the line by Cyril Knowles and Phil Beal respectively. Then, in the 56th minute, Chivers sent a powerful header past Phil Parkes to stun the home supporters. But it took Wolves just four minutes to pull level with Jim McCalliog sliding the ball past Pat Jennings following a quickly-taken free-kick from Danny Hegan. Spurs seemed happy to protect the draw and it was all home attack in the dying stages with Jennings making a fine save to prevent a John Pratt own-goal and Derek Dougan firing inches wide. Then, with just three minutes remaining, Chivers struck again with a 25-yard shot that flew into the net. Most neutrals regarded Wolves as the better side over the two legs but Spurs went 3-1 up on aggregate in the 29th minute of the return at White Hart Lane through skipper Alan Mullery. But Dave Wagstaffe, with a wonderful left-foot drive, put Wanderers back in contention shortly before the break. Despite pressing hard after the interval, there was to be no reprieve for Bill McGarry's team and after the game the Wolves boss said: "I can't work out how you can be the better side in both games and still lose." His counterpart Bill Nicholson added: "You've got to give Wolves a lot of credit. We were never really in control of this match but the important thing is we are back in Europe." The second leg was afforded just 30 minutes of highlights by ATV Midlands.

ROUTE TO THE FINAL

Round/scorers	Opponents/venue	Score
Round 1 (1).......Academica Coimbra (h)		3-0
McAlle, Richards, Dougan		
Round 1 (2).......Academica Coimbra (a)		4-1
McAlle, Dougan 3		
Round 2 (1).......Den Haag (a)		3-0
McCalliog, Dougan, Hibbitt		
Round 2 (2).......Den Haag (h)		4-0
Dougan, Weiner og, Mansveld og, Van Den Burgh og		
Round 3 (1).......Carl Zeiss Jena (a)		1-0
Richards		
Round 3 (2).......Carl Zeiss Jena (h)		3-0
Hibbitt, Dougan 2		
Round 4 (1).......Juventus (a)		1-1
McCalliog		
Round 4 (2).......Juventus (h)		2-1
Hegan, Dougan		
Semi-final (1)....Ferencvaros (a)		2-2
Munro, Richards		
Semi-final (2)....Ferencvaros (h)		2-1
Munro, Daley		
Final (1)............Tottenham Hotspur (h)		1-2
McCalliog	*Attendance: 38,362*	
Final (2)............Tottenham Hotspur (a)		1-1
Wagstaffe	*Attendance: 52,891*	

Wolves team for both legs: Parkes, Shaw, Taylor, Hegan, Munro, McAlle, McCalliog, Hibbitt, Richards, Dougan, Wagstaffe. Mike Bailey was a substitute for Hibbitt and Hugh Curran for Derek Dougan in the second leg.

INSTANT SUCCESS FOR RESERVES

Wolves' first venture into reserve football came in 1891 when a team was entered in the Shropshire League. The Molineux team proved to be a little too strong for the division, however, winning 15 and drawing one of the 16 games played over the season with a goal tally of 84 against just nine conceded. The following season interest switched to the Birmingham and District League and, once again, the second string finished the term as champions.

SOUTH AFRICA

In the 50s, Wolves twice went on tours to South Africa and the combined record for the two trips is played 20, won 20. In the first tour, which took place in May and June 1951, the 12 games saw Wolves score 50 goals and concede just five with the 13-0 trouncing of Eastern Transvaal the biggest victory – whilst Natal and a South African XI restricted the visitors' winning margins to one goal. In May 1957, an eight-game tour ended with a 10-1 rout of Southern Rhodesia followed by an 11-1 beating of Northern Rhodesia just two days later. It meant that Wanderers had scored 49 goals whilst conceding nine. A South African XI visited Molineux in September 1953, to mark the opening of the floodlights at the ground. Wolves won that one by 3-1 and a Des Horne goal was enough to decide a 1958 encounter when the South Africans again sent over a select team to Wolverhampton. Ironically, Horne was a South African.

FLOODLIT FRIENDLIES

The success of Wolves' series of floodlit friendlies earned the club world renown and was seen as the catalyst of European competition. The full list of home games in the 50s and early 60s is:

Date/scorers	Opponents	Score
30/09/53	South African XI	3-1
Mullen, Broadbent, Swinbourne		
14/10/53	Celtic	2-0
Wilshaw 2		

10/03/54 .... Racing Club of Buenos Aires 3-1
Taylor, Deeley, Mullen
13/10/54 .... First Vienna 0-0
28/10/54 .... Maccabi (Tel Aviv) 10-0
Swinbourne 3, Hancocks 2, Broadbent 2, Flowers, Wilshaw, McDonald
16/11/54 .... Moscow Spartak 4-0
Hancocks 2, Swinbourne, Wilshaw
13/12/54 .... Honved 3-2
Hancocks pen, Swinbourne 2
09/11/55 .... Moscow Dynamo 2-1
Slater, Mullen
28/01/56 .... San Lorenzo 5-1
Broadbent 3, Swinbourne, Wilshaw
29/10/56 .... Bucharest CCA 5-0
Murray 2, Hooper pen, Broadbent, Booth
11/12/56 .... Red Banner 1-1
Neil
27/03/57 .... Borussia Dortmund 4-3
Broadbent, Murray, Wilshaw, Hooper
10/04/57 .... Valencia 3-0
Thomson 2, Clamp
17/10/57 .... Real Madrid 3-2
Broadbent, Murray, Wilshaw
29/09/58 .... South African XI 1-0
Horne
10/11/60 .... Tbilisi Dynamo 5-5
Farmer 2, Murray, Mason, Durandt
03/12/62 .... Honved 1-1
Hinton

TRY AGAIN

In February 1890, Wolves and Stoke City met in an FA Cup tie at
Molineux. Wolves won by 4-0 but Stoke officials lodged a complaint
about the state of the pitch which had been subject to heavy rainfall.
The FA upheld the protest and the game was replayed a week later.
Wolves won again, doubling the original score to 8-0 – Jack Brodie
netting five of them.

FIVE MEETINGS

In March 1937, Wolves met Sunderland no fewer than five times in only 24 days. They drew 1-1 in the sixth round of the FA Cup at Molineux on March 6, and 2-2 at Roker Park four days later. Sunderland won the second replay 4-0 at Hillsborough on March 15, then, on March 26, the Black Cats hammered Wolves 6-2 in the First Division clash on Wearside and the sides drew 1-1 at Molineux three days later. Wolves and Villa met five times in the 1964/65 season – twice in the League and three times in the FA Cup, which was also the case when they played Coventry five times in 1983/84. Wolves met the Albion five times in the 2006/07 season – twice in the Championship, once in the FA Cup and twice in the Championship Play-Off semi-final.

LEAGUE CUP FINAL 1974

After the heartbreak of 1973 – when both the FA Cup and League Cup semi-finals were lost by the narrowest of margins – Wolves finally made it back to Wembley after a 14-year absence when they won through to the final of the League Cup in 1974. The route through to the Twin Towers had been somewhat bizarre with two of the ties – against Exeter City and Liverpool – taking place on midweek afternoons because of the power crisis that had gripped the country, brought about by the coal miners' strike. After a closely-fought semi-final with Norwich City, in which John Richards scored in both legs to give Wolves a 2-1 aggregate margin over the Canaries, a powerful Manchester City team lay in wait at the national stadium. City were out-and-out favourites with the bookies and, with Wolves' regular keeper Phil Parkes ruled out through injury, in came Gary Pierce who had played just 13 games for the club since his transfer from Huddersfield. Pierce celebrated his 23rd birthday at Wembley on the day of the final and he did so in the finest of fashions with a string of athletic saves to deny the likes of Rodney Marsh, Mike Summerbee, Colin Bell, Francis Lee and the great Denis Law. Both sides offered some attractive attacking football to the near-98,000 crowd and it was Wolves that made the breakthrough two minutes before the interval when

Kenny Hibbitt spectacularly volleyed home Geoff Palmer's cross. Hibbitt, as honest on the field as off it, admitted after the game that he had mis-hit the ball. Bell finally broke through Pierce's rearguard heroics in the 59th minute when he turned in a low cross from Marsh, but five minutes from time Richards steered the ball past City keeper Keith McRae in front of the end of the ground packed with gold and black clad supporters after Alan Sunderland's low centre had taken a slight deflection off Marsh on the way through to the Wolves centre-forward. Richards almost didn't make the game through a stomach injury and he was destined to miss the rest of that season through the condition. Had Dave Wagstaffe not suffered a muscle strain shortly before the winning goal was struck, Richards was in line to be replaced by substitute Barry Powell. But fate played a hand and JR played through the pain to grab glory at Wembley. The route to Wembley began in round two at Halifax:

Round/scorers	*Opponents/venue*	*Score*
Round 2	Halifax Town (a)	3-0
Sunderland, Richards, Dougan		
Round 3	Tranmere Rovers (a)	1-1
Sunderland		
Replay	Tranmere Rovers (h)	2-1
Powell, Dougan		
Round 4	Exeter City (h)	5-1
Hibbitt 2, Richards 2, Dougan		
Round 5	Liverpool (h)	1-0
Richards		
Semi-Final 1	Norwich City (a)	1-1
Richards		
Semi-Final 2	Norwich City (h)	1-0
Richards		
Final	Manchester City (Wembley)	2-1
Hibbitt, Richards		

Wolves 1974 League Cup Final team: Pierce, Palmer, Parkin, Bailey, Munro, McAlle, Hibbitt, Sunderland, Richards, Dougan, Wagstaffe (Powell).

BULLY

The man destined to become the greatest goalscorer in the long and eventful history of Wolverhampton Wanderers was born in Tipton on March 28, 1965. Steve Bull first played football for his school teams – Ocker Hill Infants and then Willingsworth High School – as well as for two local junior teams, Red Lion and Newey Goodman. He joined Tipton Town after leaving school and his goalscoring exploits for them were noted by one of West Bromwich's scouts and he signed professional forms for the Albion in August 1985. In nine games for the Baggies he scored three goals before, on November 20, 1986, he came to Molineux along with Andy Thompson in a deal set up by Graham Turner. Steve made his debut against Wrexham just two days later in a Wolves side that was struggling in the mid-table region of the Fourth Division and a crowd of just over 5,000 at Molineux saw them go down 3-0 in a dismal and depressing game. Worse was to come on the following Monday evening as the cup-tied Bull was forced to watch from the stand as Wolves suffered the worst humiliation in their history when they crashed out of the FA Cup to non-League Chorley. He came straight back into the team and scored his first goal for the club in early December in a Freight Rover Trophy game at Cardiff. Then, 11 days later, he got his first League goal in a 1-0 win at Hartlepool. Steve got another five goals in 11 matches before the game at the beginning of February 1987, against Stockport at Molineux, which many people saw as the turning point for the club. Wolves were one down with less than 15 minutes to go when they suddenly found their form and scored three with Steve Bull one of the goalgetters. Wanderers then lost only three of the 22 games they played in the remainder of the season. They just missed out on promotion and then lost the Play-Off final to Aldershot. Bull scored 11 goals in those games, giving him a total of 19 in his first season at Molineux. In the final League game he got his first hat-trick for Wanderers in a 4-1 home victory over Hartlepool. Steve had started to win many admirers, but in season 1987/88 he was to become a cult hero as Wolves stormed to the Fourth Division Championship and also enjoyed a trip to Wembley where they beat Burnley to win the Sherpa Van Trophy. Bull scored 34

STEVE BULL CASTS A PREDATORY EYE OVER ANDY MUTCH'S NUMBER NINE SHIRT

league goals; three in the FA Cup, three in the Littlewoods Cup and 12 in the Sherpa Van Trophy giving him an incredible total of 52. He was the first player to score 50 League and cup goals in an English season since Peterborough's Terry Bly almost 30 years earlier. The following season saw him score four hat-tricks and two four-goal hauls as Wolves swept to the Third Division title and came within a whisker of a Wembley return. This time he ended the term with 50 goals. The last time any player had scored 50 in two consecutive seasons was Middlesbrough's George Camsell in the mid-1920s. Bull's goalscoring exploits led to him being chosen to play for his country, firstly at Under-21 level, then, in May 1989, at full level when he came on as a substitute at Hampden Park and smashed in a goal against the Scots to help silence the critics who had claimed that he could only score in the lower leagues. In April, 1990, he scored two against Czechoslovakia at Wembley to clinch a place on the plane to Italy for the World Cup Finals. In all he won 13 full caps, eight of them after coming on as substitute, and he scored four goals. He also made five appearances for the England B team. In 1992, Bull broke the Wolves goalscoring record – set by former Molineux idol John Richards – when he netted his 195th goal for the club that he always remained loyal to after resisting the temptation to join sides in the Premiership on several occasions. In February 1998, he scored his 300th goal for Wolves, and six months later he notched his 18th hat-trick for the side in a game against Barnet. But a knee injury that failed to respond to surgery forced him to hang up his boots in the summer of 1999 at the age of 35. He returned to the field of play to make several appearances for Conference League Hereford United the following season before quitting again and concentrating on his work at Molineux in a PR capacity. His loyalty to Wolves, his goal scoring exploits and charity work contributed to Bully, as he is still affectionately known by the fans, being awarded the MBE in the Millennium New Year's honours list. In 2003, the John Ireland Stand was renamed the Steve Bull Stand and, in July 2006, Steve was made honorary Vice-President of Wolves. That month, the pre-season home friendly against Aston Villa was designated Bully's 20th anniversary game – Steve made his final appearance in gold and black, playing the first five minutes of the match.

AMERICAN SUCCESS

After securing a place back in football's top-flight in 1967, the team took on the guise of Los Angeles Wolves for a prestigious soccer tournament in America. It proved to be a successful crossing of the Atlantic with Ronnie Allen's men making it through to the final where they beat Aberdeen – who represented Washington – in an incredible game that finished at 6-5 after 130 minutes' play. After an opening draw against Bangu of Brazil, Wolves beat the Uruguayans of Cerro 2-0 before another draw, this time against Stoke City. Consecutive wins against Hibernian (2-1), Sunderland (5-1) and Glentoran (4-0) followed, then came a drawn game with Aberdeen which was later ordered to be replayed as Wolves had used three substitutes instead of the permitted two. After another draw, this time against Shamrock Rovers, Wanderers lost for the first time in the tournament when they went down 1-0 to ADO The Hague in a bad-tempered affair that saw three players sent off; Derek Dougan and Ernie Hunt the Wolves men to be banished. The sides met again three days later and revenge proved to be sweet thanks to a 2-0 Wolves win. Draws against Cagliari and Dundee United came before the replayed game against Aberdeen. Although the Scots won 3-0, Wolves had done enough to earn a place in the final which was played at the Los Angeles Coliseum in front of a 17,824 crowd. Down 2-1 at the interval after Peter Knowles had opened the scoring, Wolves hit back to take the lead after an amazing spell directly after the interval which saw Dave Burnside netting a hat-trick while Jim Storrie was on target for Aberdeen. And 4-3 was the way it stayed until the final minute when Frank Munro, who was shortly to sign for Wolves, levelled matters from the penalty spot. Dougan made it 5-4 23 minutes into extra-time and then Terry Wharton saw his penalty saved. It proved to be costly as play swept straight to the other end and, with the referee about to blow for time, Aberdeen were awarded another penalty with Munro, once again, making no mistake. Play then moved into 'sudden death' mode and after 10 minutes Ally Shewan attempted to hook clear Bobby Thomson's cross but he succeeded only in helping the ball past his own keeper.

ALL GOLD

A surprise lay in store for the near-48,000 crowd that were at Molineux to watch a fifth-round FA Cup replay against Aston Villa on February 24, 1965. For when Wolves ran out they were wearing a matching strip with gold shorts, complete with numbers, replacing the traditional black ones. The game finished goalless although Wanderers did go on to win the second replay. The club reverted to black shorts after Bill McGarry had taken over as boss and the more familiar kit made its return at Goodison Park on January 28, 1969, when Everton rattled in four goals without reply – the all-gold outfit having made its final appearance in the FA Cup defeat at Tottenham Hotspur three days earlier.

TEN-GOAL FRIENDLY DRAW

Wolves have never drawn a League game 5-5 but they did share 10 goals in a friendly with Tbilisi Dynamo at Molineux in November 1960. Wolves trailed 5-2 with 12 minutes to go but goals from Cliff Durandt, Ted Farmer and Jimmy Murray spared their blushes. Farmer had also scored in the first half which ended with Wolves going in to the break 3-1 down. Bobby Mason reduced the arrears further on 60 minutes before the Russians struck twice more. Then came the late fightback.

SWIFT RETURN

Relegation to the Second Division in 1976 cost Bill McGarry his job as Wolves' manager. McGarry's number two through his eight seasons at the helm at Molineux was Sammy Chung and he took over the managerial reins, steering Wanderers to an instant return to the First Division. Chung managed to retain all of the relegated side and they proved to be a force to be reckoned with, losing just seven games during the campaign. Consistency was the keyword with four of the squad – Gary Pierce, Steve Daley, Geoff Palmer and Derek Parkin – ever-presents. Added to that, Alan Sunderland, John McAlle and Kenny Hibbitt missed just six games between them. John Richards missed the first third of the season through injury but when he returned he hit 20 League and Cup goals to finish as top scorer, two in front of Hibbitt. The final home match was against Chelsea and the one-all draw meant that Wolves finished as champions and Chelsea were assured of promotion. A week later, a goal from Hibbitt at Bolton prevented promotion for the home side and allowed Brian Clough's Nottingham Forest to take third place. The following year, the East Midlands club won the Championship and League Cup and that was followed by consecutive European Cup triumphs as well as another League Cup Final victory. Forest made it through to the 1980 League Cup Final too but their hopes of a third win in three years were stopped at Wembley by Andy Gray's goal for Wolves.

FOOTBALL LEAGUE DIVISION TWO

		Pl	W	D	L	F	A	W	D	L	F	A	Pts
1	WOLVES	42	15	3	3	48	21	7	10	4	36	24	57
2	Chelsea	42	15	6	0	51	22	6	7	8	22	31	55
3	Nottingham Forest	42	14	3	4	53	22	7	7	7	24	21	52
4	Bolton Wanderers	42	15	2	4	46	21	5	9	7	29	33	51
5	Blackpool	42	11	7	3	29	17	6	10	5	29	25	51
6	Luton Town	42	13	5	3	39	17	8	1	12	28	31	48
7	Charlton Athletic	42	14	5	2	52	27	2	11	8	19	31	48
8	Notts County	42	11	5	5	29	20	8	5	8	36	40	48
9	Southampton	42	12	6	3	40	24	5	4	12	32	43	44
10	Millwall	42	9	6	6	31	22	6	7	8	26	31	43
11	Sheffield United	42	9	8	4	32	25	5	4	12	22	38	40
12	Blackburn Rovers	42	12	4	5	31	18	3	5	13	11	36	39
13	Oldham Athletic	42	11	6	4	37	23	3	4	14	15	41	38
14	Hull City	42	9	8	4	31	17	1	9	11	14	36	37
15	Bristol Rovers	42	8	9	4	32	27	4	4	13	21	41	37
16	Burnley	42	8	9	4	27	20	3	5	13	19	44	36
17	Fulham	42	9	7	5	39	25	2	6	13	15	36	35
18	Cardiff City	42	7	6	8	30	30	5	4	12	26	37	34
19	Leyton Orient	42	4	8	9	18	23	5	8	8	19	32	34
20	Carlisle United	42	7	7	7	31	33	4	5	12	18	42	34
21	Plymouth Argyle	42	5	9	7	27	25	3	7	11	19	40	32
22	Hereford United	42	6	9	6	28	30	2	6	13	29	48	31

DOUBLE AGONY

Wolves came within a single point of being the first team to do the League and Cup double since Aston Villa did it in 1897. A week before they took part in the 1960 FA Cup Final, Wanderers enjoyed a 5-1 victory over Chelsea at Stamford Bridge to head the table by a point from Burnley. On the same afternoon, the Clarets shared the spoils with Fulham in a goal-less encounter at Turf Moor. But the Lancashire side had a game left to play, at Manchester City two days later, and the 2-1 win they secured at Maine Road was enough for them to leapfrog Wolves and take the title. All the goals came in the first 31 minutes with City's Clive Colbridge cancelling out Burnley's opener which came after four minutes when home keeper Bert Trautmann deflected in Brian Pilkington's low cross. Then came what proved to be the winner from Trevor Meredith. Ironically, it was the first time Burnley had sat at the top of the table in the whole campaign. Wolves, who had a vastly superior goal average, were left rueing the home slip-up against Spurs in the penultimate game of the season and, whilst they had the consolation of Wembley glory over Blackburn Rovers, the players and supporters must have been sickened by the knowledge that one point cost a third consecutive Championship – and the double.

LOST BALL

As Wolves closed in on promotion to the First Division in February 1967, they came out on top of a thriller against Portsmouth at Fratton Park by 3-2. One of the scorers was Peter Knowles, who celebrated his goal by retrieving the ball from the back of the net and booting it out of the ground. Pompey officials were none too impressed and they sent Knowles the bill for a new ball.

DEADLY DENNIS

Centre-forward Dennis Westcott hit the highest League total for Wolves in 1946/47 when he netted 38 from just 35 games. He scored a hat-trick against Liverpool at Anfield in just eight minutes in December of that campaign and, following the turn of the year, he was on target in 14 of 16 League games he participated in.

GROUND CLOSED

As a result of crowd misbehaviour, Molineux was closed for two games shortly after the end of the First World War. In a game against Bury in October 1919, the referee – a Mr Lowe – awarded a penalty to the Lancashire club who were already a goal up. It was a controversial decision which, after several others beforehand, proved to be the last straw for several members of the crowd who invaded the pitch and gave chase to the unfortunate official who lost momentum in his haste to reach the dressing-rooms and fell over. The players came to his aid before the crowd could reach him and, although the match continued after order had been restored with Bury winning 1-0, the Football League closed Molineux for two games. They were against Barnsley and Stockport County and both were played at West Bromwich. Luck was certainly against Wanderers in the first of the encounters as they lost goalkeeper Teddy Peers – injured as Barnsley opened the scoring. Later the 'guest' home side also lost the services of winger Billy Harrison and, on a snowy afternoon at The Hawthorns, the nine men went down by 4-2. The game against County the following week ended in a two-all draw.

LEAGUE CUP 1980

Just as in their first League Cup Final against Manchester City in 1974, Wolves were very much the underdogs when they came up against Brian Clough's Nottingham Forest at Wembley in March 1980. Not only had Forest won the trophy in the two previous seasons, but they were also reigning European Cup holders and had finished as Football League runners-up at the end of the 1978/79 campaign. Although only one of the five teams that Wolves met on the way to the final was from the top flight, it was a far from easy journey for Bill McGarry's team. In the quarter-final it was only at the third attempt that Grimsby Town were overcome. The Mariners at least had the consolation of finishing as Third Division Champions at the end of the season. Wolves then had to come from behind in the semi-final to see off the challenge of Swindon Town, another Division Three club who took a 2-1 first-leg advantage to Molineux. It took a late goal from John Richards as Town were finally beaten 3-1 to eventually decide who was going to Wembley. In the final the only goal came midway through the second period following an awful mix-up between Forest keeper Peter Shilton and defender David Needham who both missed Peter Daniel's long ball allowing Andy Gray the simplest of tasks in converting into an empty net. The east Midlanders threw everything at Paul Bradshaw's goal in the closing stages in an effort to gain an equaliser, but Emlyn Hughes, using his vast experience, marshalled his defence superbly and Wolves held out. Four team members – Geoff Palmer, Derek Parkin, John Richards and Kenny Hibbitt – also played in the 1974 League Cup success. The route to the Final:

Round/scorers	*Opponents/venue*	*Score*
Round 2 (1)	Burnley (a)	1-1
Palmer		
Round 2 (2)	Burnley (h)	2-0
Palmer, Hibbitt		
Round 3	Crystal Palace (a)	1-0
Hibbitt		
Round 4	Queens Park Rangers (h)	1-0
Carr		
Round 5	Grimsby Town (a)	0-0
Round 5 replay	Grimsby Town (h)	1-1
Gray		
Second replay	Grimsby Town (The Baseball Ground)	2-0
Richards, Hibbitt		
Semi-final (1)	Swindon Town (a)	1-2
Daniel		
Semi-final (2)	Swindon Town (h)	3-1
Richards 2, Eves		
Final	Nottingham Forest (at Wembley)	1-0
Gray		

Wolves 1980 League Cup Final team: Bradshaw, Palmer, Parkin, Daniel, Berry, Hughes, Hibbitt, Carr, Gray, Richards, Eves. Unused sub: Brazier.

MATCHWINNER ANDY GRAY AFTER THE 1980 LEAGUE CUP TRIUMPH OVER NOTTINGHAM FOREST

NUMBER NINE

Wolves have been blessed with some of the finest centre-forwards the game could offer over the years. Names like Tom Phillipson, Billy Hartill, Dennis Westcott, Jimmy Murray, Derek Dougan, John Richards and Steve Bull spring readily to mind. But whilst the first player to wear a number nine shirt at Molineux was one of the game's greats, he wasn't a Wolves man. It was the legendary Dixie Dean of Everton and England. Everton had won the FA Cup, beating Manchester City 3-0 at Wembley on April 29, 1933, and it was the first time numbers were worn in that prestige game, Everton sporting 1 to 11 and City 12 to 22. A week later, May 6, the cup winners came to Molineux for the final League match of the season and wore their Cup Final strip, Dean carrying the number nine on his back. Wolves won 4-2 to ensure they avoided relegation in their first season back in the top-flight. On target that day were Mark Crook, Jack Hetherington (with two) and Charlie Phillips whilst Dean failed to mark the occasion with a goal for himself. It was not, however, the first time numbers had been worn in a League game. On the opening day of the 1928/29 season Arsenal wore numbers against Sheffield Wednesday and Chelsea against Swansea. A proposal by Spurs for shirt-numbering was defeated at the Football League AGM in 1933. So, despite the logic of shirt numbers to allow fans to know who was who, it was not introduced permanently until the aborted 1939-40 season.

MONKEY GLANDS

There was considerable concern aroused by reports during the 1938/39 season that Wolves players were being given monkey gland injections to improve their stamina. The experiment was one of the many innovations tried by manager Major Frank Buckley and it prompted Leicester MP Montague Lyons to ask a question in the House of Commons calling on the Minister of Health to order an official investigation into the matter. The MP may have been prompted by Leicester's dismissal from that season's FA Cup at the hands of Wolves! But legend has it that the injections contained little more than anti-flu vaccine.

GIVING BURNLEY THE BLUES

Between 1964 and 2003, Wolves played Burnley at Turf Moor in 15 League matches and didn't taste defeat once. Over the 39-year period Wolves won 10 and drew five of the games at the Lancashire venue, scoring 32 goals and conceding 14 before the run finally ended with a 2-1 reversal on Boxing Day 2003.

COTTAGERS CRUMBLE

Bob Pennington of the *Daily Express* began his match report on Wolves' 9-0 thrashing of Fulham with: 'This was a massacre without mercy, revenge without even a tinge of compassion'. Just a week earlier, in September 1959, the reigning League Champions had suffered their first reversal of the campaign when newly-promoted Fulham won 3-1 on the banks of the Thames. Three up at the break, Wolves continued to pound the visiting defence who conceded a fourth in the 58th minute when Peter Broadbent steered the ball past goalkeeper Tony Macedo. That was the first of a five-goal burst in a 15-minute spell. Norman Deeley completed the rout shortly before the end when he netted his fourth goal of the evening although the best strike of the game award went to Ron Flowers when he scored the third. Pennington's marvellous description read: 'It was a goal so fantastically fast you needed a slow-motion camera to catch a trace of it. There stood Flowers a good 30 yards from the Fulham goal. Up went his left boot followed by a tremendous crunch of tortured leather. All the human eye could catch was a white blur, a flashing red jersey, and Young England goalkeeper Tony Macedo clawing at the air with the ball behind him, distending the white netting.' Credit went to the Fulham players at the end of the game when they stayed on to applaud the Wolves players off the pitch.

BILLY'S RETURN

Billy Wright's first visit to Molineux in an 'official' capacity following his retirement as a player didn't prove to be a happy one. It was on April 8, 1963, as manager of Arsenal that he returned to the scene of so many former glories. But Terry Wharton's 64th-minute goal sent Billy and the Gunners back to Highbury pointless.

FIVE TIMERS

Three men have scored five in League games for Wolves. Joe Butcher was the first to achieve the feat in a game against Accrington in November 1892. Wolves won 5-3 and sympathies that afternoon would have been extended to John Kirkham of Accrington who scored a hat-trick which meant that just two men scored the game's eight goals. Tom Phillipson's gift to the fans on Christmas Day 1926 was five goals in a 7-2 win over Bradford City. Billy Hartill hit five on two occasions – against Notts County in a 5-1 win in October 1929, and then he was the only scorer against Aston Villa who slipped to a 5-0 defeat in September 1934. All four games were played at Molineux, as was the FA Cup tie with Stoke City in February 1890, when Jack Brodie became the only man to hit five for Wolves in a cup game. Wanderers won that quarter-final tie by 8-0.

GUNNERS SHOT DOWN I

Five of the starting line-up that faced Arsenal at Molineux in the first post-war First Division game in August 1946, had played in the final match of the 1938/39 term – the last complete season before hostilities began. Bill Morris, Stan Cullis, Jimmy Mullen, Tom Galley and Dennis Westcott were the names familiar to the home fans in the 50,845 crowd. Angus McLean had been a regular in wartime football for Wolves, while Bert Williams and Fred Ramscar had played in the Football League South campaign of 1945/46. Making their debut against the Gunners were Jesse Pye and Johnny Hancocks and they made an instant impression as Wanderers hit the north London side for six and conceded just one in the process. Pye helped himself to a hat-trick, Westcott netted two and Mullen was also on target with Hancocks having a hand in the first two goals. Oddly, at the interval the game was scoreless.

UNCONVINCING

Following relegation to the Second Division in 1982, Wolves, under the new ownership of Allied Properties, made an instant return to the top flight finishing the term as runners up to Queens Park Rangers. But, despite an impressive start which saw just one goal conceded in an unbeaten spell of nine games that yielded 21 points, form became more erratic as the season wore on and from a position where the title looked odds-on, a run of just four wins from the final 17 games handed the honour to Queens Park Rangers. True, only three games were lost in that run but 10 draws limited the points intake. A measure of the team's inconsistency came on the afternoon they secured promotion. Playing against Charlton Athletic at The Valley, a three-goal lead was surrendered as the Londoners fought back to take a point. Veteran goalkeeper John Burridge and full-back John Humphrey played in all 46 League and Cup games, with Mel Eves ending the campaign as leading scorer with 19 goals.

FOOTBALL LEAGUE DIVISION TWO

		Pl	W	D	L	F	A	W	D	L	F	A	Pts
1	Queens Park Rangers	42	16	3	2	51	16	10	4	7	26	20	85
2	WOLVES	42	14	5	2	42	16	6	10	5	26	28	75
3	Leicester City	42	11	4	6	36	15	9	6	6	36	29	70
4	Fulham	42	13	5	3	36	20	7	4	10	28	27	69
5	Newcastle United	42	13	6	2	43	21	5	7	9	32	32	67
6	Sheffield Wednesday	42	9	8	4	33	23	7	7	7	27	24	63
7	Oldham Athletic	42	8	10	3	38	24	6	9	6	26	23	61
8	Leeds United	42	7	11	3	28	22	6	10	5	23	24	60
9	Shrewsbury Town	42	8	9	4	20	15	7	5	9	28	33	59
10	Barnsley	42	9	8	4	37	28	5	7	9	20	27	57
11	Blackburn Rovers	42	11	7	3	38	21	4	5	12	20	37	57
12	Cambridge United	42	11	7	3	26	17	2	5	14	16	43	51
13	Derby County	42	7	10	4	27	24	3	9	9	22	34	49
14	Carlisle United	42	10	6	5	44	28	2	6	13	24	42	48
15	Crystal Palace	42	11	7	3	31	17	1	5	15	12	35	48
16	Middlesbrough	42	8	7	6	27	29	3	8	10	19	38	48
17	Charlton Athletic	42	11	3	7	40	31	2	6	13	23	55	48
18	Chelsea	42	8	8	5	31	22	3	6	12	20	39	47
19	Grimsby Town	42	9	7	5	32	26	3	4	14	13	44	47
20	Rotherham United	42	6	7	8	22	29	4	8	9	23	39	45
21	Burnley	42	10	4	7	38	24	2	4	15	18	42	44
22	Bolton Wanderers	42	10	2	9	30	26	1	9	11	12	35	44

FIRST OFF

The first Wolves player to take an early bath in a League fixture was goalkeeper Tom Baddeley who was dismissed, reportedly, for kicking Nottingham Forest centre-forward Fred Lessons in a fixture at the Town Ground on New Year's Eve in 1904. The referee that afternoon was a Mr D. G. Ashworth and the 10 men held out for a two-all draw. But, 14 years earlier, in January 1890, Ted Tomkyes was sent off in a Staffordshire Senior Cup first round tie against Great Bridge Unity for fighting with a member of the opposition. He is believed to be the first player to be sent off since the club's formation.

A GOOD WEEK

Although Wolves' first flirtation with the Premier League was to ultimately end in relegation in 2004, there were some high spots during the campaign; none more so than when Dave Jones' team beat Manchester United at Molineux on January 17 and then held Liverpool to a draw four days later in another home fixture. Kenny Miller's 67th-minute strike put paid to United and then the Scottish striker popped up with a last-minute equaliser against the Merseysiders, in front shortly before the interval through Bruno Cheyrou.

A BAD DAY AT THE OFFICE

On November 11, 1923, Wolves suffered one of just three defeats from a season that ended with them as champions of Division Three (North). The team slipped to a 2-0 reversal at Grimsby and, that day, the club was fined £10-10 shillings (£10.50) for paying excess bonuses to the players.

PHIL'S LONG STRETCH

Goalkeeper Phil Parkes played for a record 171 consecutive League and cup games for Wolves between September 1970 and September 1973. Included in that total are 127 League games – which is also a record.

KENNY MILLER SHOCKS MANCHESTER UNITED DURING WOLVES' BRIEF PREMIERSHIP STINT

HALFWAY THERE

At the half-way stage of the 1957/58 season, Wolves were leading the table six points ahead of their nearest rivals, West Bromwich. The similarities between Wolves' record at the half-way stage of that campaign, and the one four years earlier when they captured the title for the first time, was amazing. The totals were:

	W	D	L	F	A	Pts
1953/54	14	5	2	54	29	33
1957/58	14	5	2	56	25	33

The 1954 Champions finished four points clear of second placed West Bromwich after taking 24 points from the second half of the season whilst the 1958 team finished five points ahead of runners-up Preston North End having taken 31 points from their remaining 21 matches.

GUNNERS SHOT DOWN II

Arsenal were the double-holders when they came to Molineux in November 1971 – and when they went into the half-time break a Ray Kennedy goal to the good, the Highbury players must have imagined that things were looking good for a repeat of the previous season's 3-0 win at Wolves. But Dave Wagstaffe's spectacular 53rd-minute equaliser was the first of a five goals in 20 minutes burst from the Molineux men as a heavy snowstorm swept across the ground. Kenny Hibbitt put Wolves ahead and, before the cheering had subsided, Derek Dougan netted a third. Jim McCalliog then converted a penalty before Dougan completed the rout with a volley from just inside the penalty area.

THE FIRST STEP

After going so close in the previous campaign, Wolves were in a determined mood and they made no mistake – storming to the Fourth Division title in 1988. It was the first step on the ladder back to top-flight football although the season didn't get off to the most auspicious of starts with an opening day draw at Scarborough – who were playing their first League game – being ruined by hooligans. The first 11 games included four wins and four defeats before 12 wins and just one defeat from a 16-game run catapulted the side to the top of the table. Promotion was eventually confirmed with a 3-1 win at doomed Newport County – and the title quickly followed as a brace from Steve Bull put paid to Hartlepool at Molineux. Goalkeeper Mark Kendall and striker Andy Mutch played in each of the 61 League and Cup games played by Wolves in the season whilst Bull missed just three as he destroyed defences to amass 52 goals.

FOOTBALL LEAGUE DIVISION FOUR

		Pl	W	D	L	F	A	W	D	L	F	A	Pts
1	WOLVES	46	15	3	5	47	19	12	6	5	35	24	90
2	Cardiff City	46	15	6	2	39	14	9	7	7	27	27	85
3	Bolton Wanderers	46	15	6	2	42	12	7	6	10	24	30	78
4	Scunthorpe United	46	14	5	4	42	20	6	12	5	34	31	77
5	Torquay United	46	10	7	6	34	16	11	7	5	32	25	77
6	Swansea City	46	9	7	7	35	28	11	3	9	27	28	70
7	Peterborough United	46	10	5	8	28	26	10	5	8	24	27	70
8	Leyton Orient	46	13	4	6	55	27	6	8	9	30	36	69
9	Colchester United	46	10	5	8	23	22	9	5	9	24	29	67
10	Burnley	46	12	5	6	31	22	8	2	13	26	40	67
11	Wrexham	46	13	3	7	46	26	7	3	13	23	32	66
12	Scarborough	46	12	8	3	38	19	5	6	12	18	29	65
13	Darlington	46	13	6	4	39	25	5	5	13	32	44	65
14	Tranmere Rovers	46	14	2	7	43	20	5	7	11	18	33	64
15	Cambridge United	46	10	6	7	32	24	6	7	10	18	28	61
16	Hartlepool United	46	9	7	7	25	25	6	7	10	25	32	59
17	Crewe Alexandra	46	7	11	5	25	19	6	8	9	32	34	58
18	Halifax Town	46	11	7	5	37	25	3	7	13	17	34	55
19	Hereford United	46	8	7	8	25	27	6	5	12	16	32	54
20	Stockport County	46	7	7	9	26	26	5	8	10	18	32	53
21	Rochdale	46	5	9	9	28	34	6	6	11	19	42	48
22	Exeter City	46	8	6	9	33	29	3	7	13	20	39	46
23	Carlisle United	46	9	5	9	38	33	3	3	17	19	53	44
24	Newport County	46	4	5	14	19	36	2	2	19	16	69	25

HONVED

Of all the friendly games that Wolves have played, the one that is most frequently recalled is when the mighty Honved team came to town in 1954. After Hungary had thrashed England by 6-3 at Wembley and then 7-1 in the return in Budapest, the English game was at its lowest ebb. Six of the team that had given England a footballing lesson at Wembley a year previously, as well as a regular who missed the game through injury, were included in the Honved side. The 55,000 crowd created a tremendous atmosphere but that was muted in the 10th minute when, from a Ferenc Puskas free-kick fortuitously awarded on the edge of the box after the ball had hit Ron Flowers' hand, Sandor Kocsis headed home. Although Roy Swinbourne came close to equalising, Honved broke away and Ferencs Machos slipped the ball past Williams. Two down and the game was still in its infancy. But the team, nor for that matter the crowd, refused to yield and four minutes after the break Wolves had pulled a goal back when Johnny Hancocks ran through into the area only to be fouled by Imre Kovacs. The diminutive Wolves number seven converted the spot-kick and that was the signal for an all-out assault on the Honved goal. Such was the importance of the game, it was broadcast on radio and shown on live television. The radio commentators – in their excitement as Wolves got more and more on top – kept referring to Honved as Hungary. Molineux erupted when Swinbourne got a deserved equaliser 14 minutes from the end. Wolves had forced a succession of corners, all of which had come to nothing then Dennis Wilshaw's centre found the head of Swinbourne and, to the deafening roar of the crowd, the ball hit the back of the net. A minute later, Les Smith went on a run down the left, beat two Honved defenders and centred for Swinbourne to hook the ball home for what proved to be the winner. The following morning, Wolves commanded the headlines of the national press. 'Wolves champions of the World now' said the *Daily Mail*, whilst the *News Chronicle* led with 'That's great Wolves, another boost for England: Honved hammered'. It showed the measure of importance of the match to football in England – and Wolves had not failed in their duty.

IPSWICH FRIENDLY

On a Wednesday evening in March 1938, Major Frank Buckley kept a promise he had made earlier in that season to send a side to play Ipswich in a friendly at Portman Road. At the time, Town were in the Southern League although they were to gain entry into the Football League (South) that summer. The game, which kicked off at the unusual time of 5.30pm, finished as a two-all draw. Ambrose Mulraney hit a brace for the home team whilst Horace Wright and Dickie Dorsett found the net for Wanderers in front of a 12,600 crowd.

NIFTY NAT

Which England centre-forward three times played in goal against Wolves, never conceded a goal and even saved a penalty? Answer: Nat Lofthouse. The man nicknamed 'The Lion of Vienna' after his winning goal against Austria in 1952, first had to don the keeper's jersey for Bolton at Molineux on February 11, 1956. Debutant goalkeeper Joe Dean, just 16, had to go off to have stitches put in a cut above his eye. While he was between the posts for some 10 minutes, Lofthouse turned a Ron Flowers header neatly over the bar. His stint in goal over, he returned to his normal position to score an equaliser for Bolton but Wolves ended as 4-2 winners. Lofthouse had an even longer spell in goal at Molineux almost exactly a year later. Wolves were leading 3-0 on February 2, 1957, when England international Eddie Hopkinson broke a finger. Into goal went Lofthouse once again and not only did he keep a clean sheet as the Lancashire side pulled back to 3-2, he even saved a Harry Hooper penalty in the last few seconds. When Bolton, as cup holders, met League champions Wolves in the Charity Shield at Burnden Park on October 5, 1958, Lofthouse yet again turned shot-stopper. Dean dislocated his shoulder after 10 minutes and Lofthouse had a 14-minute spell in the green jersey before Hopkinson, who had been watching the game from the stands, was able to get changed and substitute for Dean. Again Wolves failed to beat the England centre-forward who was later twice on target as Bolton took the trophy 4-1.

GOLDEN JUBILEE

To mark the Football League's 50th anniversary, a series of Jubilee Fund games were played to raise cash for former players who had fallen on hard times. Wolves played Stoke at the start of the 1938/39 season and won 4-3 at Molineux with goals from Reg Kirkham (two), Dickie Dorsett and Teddy Maguire. At the start of the following campaign, which was to be aborted after the outbreak of the Second World War, Wolves won the return game 4-2 at the Victoria Ground with Dorsett hitting a hat-trick.

MOST INTERNATIONAL CAPS WITH WOLVES

England ....Billy Wright; 90 as captain, 1939 to 1959 105
Scotland ....Kenny Miller, 2001 to 2006 25
Wales ....Wayne Hennessey, 2007 onwards................... 29
Northern Ireland ......Derek Dougan, 1966 to 1975 26
Republic of Ireland ...Andy Keogh, 2007 onwards............................ 17

A DARK NIGHT

Bolton made it a miserable Christmas for Wolves in 1959. After winning 2-1 at Burnden Park on Boxing Day, the Lancashire side then became the first team to beat Wolves under the Molineux floodlights in the return two days later – Brian Birch getting the only goal of the game two minutes after the interval. Wolves paid the ultimate price after squandering numerous chances although their cause wasn't helped when they lost the services of Eddie Stuart with a pulled muscle whilst goalkeeper Malcolm Finlayson hobbled around his area with a knee injury after a collision.

GOAL FEASTS

It wasn't only the first team that was in a goalscoring frame of mind on October 7, 1961. At Molineux the reserves were clocking up a 7-1 win over Manchester City with Ted Farmer grabbing a hat-trick. Over at St. Andrew's the senior side hammered the Blues by 6-3 – among the scorers Mark Lazarus, notching his first goal for Wanderers.

DOUBLE RED

Sunderland found themselves up against it when they visited Molineux in December 1991. The Black Cats were reduced to just nine men in the opening minutes following a double sending-off. First to go was John Byrne after eight minutes and, three minutes later, he was joined in the dressing-room by Gordon Armstrong. Both men were red-carded by Coventry referee Keren Barratt for allegedly making comments to a linesman. The nine remaining players fought tooth and nail, however, and it wasn't until the 82nd minute that Paul Cook volleyed home the game's only goal to win it for Wolves.

CENTENARY FESTIVAL

On the weekend of April 16 and 17, 1988, Wolves were invited to compete for the Football League's Centenary Festival Trophy at Wembley Stadium. Sixteen teams took part and the games were played on a knockout basis of 40 minutes' duration. Wolves, then in the Fourth Division, were drawn against Everton who were the reigning League Champions. After just three minutes, former Wolf Wayne Clarke gave the Merseysiders the lead but that was cancelled out by what many regarded the best goal of the weekend – a 25-yard rocket shot from Robbie Dennison with just five minutes remaining. The game went to a penalty shoot-out and, with the score at 2-2, Gary Bellamy was presented with the chance of winning it for Wolves only for Everton keeper Neville Southall to save. Alan Harper then converted for the Toffees and, when Andy Mutch missed with his kick, Wolves were out. In the final, Nottingham Forest beat Sheffield Wednesday by 3-2 in a penalty decider after a goalless draw.

BIG GAME BOGEY

Tottenham Hotspur certainly seem to have some kind of spell over Wolves when it comes to big games. The Londoners have beaten Wanderers in the 1921 FA Cup Final, the 1972 UEFA Cup Final, the 1973 League Cup semi-final and the 1981 FA Cup semi-final.

EVERYTHING TO PLAY FOR

There was plenty at stake and Molineux was bursting at the seams when Wolves met Liverpool on Tuesday May 4, 1976. The Reds needed the two points to wrest the Championship title away from Queens Park Rangers whilst Wolves needed a win – and a Birmingham defeat at Sheffield United – to maintain their First Division status. Both games were played on the same evening. And, at half-time, it was all looking good. Steve Kindon had fired Wolves into a ninth-minute lead and the Blades were a goal up against Birmingham. But three goals from the Merseysiders in the last 20 minutes – from Ray Kennedy, Kevin Keegan and John Toshack – condemned Wolves to the drop and gave the Anfield team the title. The result mattered not for the home team, however, as Birmingham equalised at Bramall Lane to take the point that would have given them safety regardless of the outcome at Molineux.

WHAT A SEASON

The Molineux trophy cabinet was filled near to capacity in 1958 after an incredible season finished with all four levels of Wolves' teams having won their respective Leagues. The first team captured the League Championship, the reserves the Central League, the third team finished top of the Birmingham League and the fourth team took the Worcestershire Combination title and the Worcestershire Combination Challenge Cup. Added to that the club's juniors won the FA Youth Cup. The only substantial piece of silverware missing that year was the FA Cup. Wolves lost at the quarter-final stage by 2-1 at Bolton where they lay siege to the Trotters' goal but couldn't get the equaliser that would have been the very least their efforts deserved from the game.

THE SHERPA VAN TROPHY

With the Fourth Division Championship already in the bag in 1988, Wolves gave their supporters double cause to celebrate by winning the Sherpa Van Trophy in front of an 80,000 crowd at Wembley. The competition was for Third and Fourth

Division clubs with Burnley, the other finalist, like Wolves, founder members of the Football League. Just 2886 watched the preliminary round meeting between Swansea and Wolves at the Vetch Field and only two of the seven matches involving the Molineux team leading up to the final boasted crowds of five figures. After the decline of the club under the reign of the Bhatti brothers in the 80s, Wembley must have seemed a million miles away to the Wolves faithful but, on that Whit Bank Holiday Sunday, the sun shone and goals from Andy Mutch and Robbie Dennison capped a fine performance and victory. Perhaps the only real surprise of the afternoon was that Steve Bull didn't score. He had an assist in Mutch's 23rd-minute opener but he couldn't add to his tally of 12 goals in the competition that season having scored in every round leading up to Wembley. Dennison's goal was a superbly executed free-kick six minutes into the second half.

Round/scorers	*Opponents/venue*	*Score*
Prelim. Round	Swansea City (a)	1-1
Bull		
Prelim. Round	Bristol City (h)	3-1
Vaughan, Bull 2		
Round 1	Brentford (h)	4-0
Bull 3, Dennison		
Round 2	Peterborough United (h)	4-0
Dennison, Bull 2, Mutch		
Round 3	Torquay United (h)	1-0
Bull		
Area Final (1)	Notts County (a)	1-1
Bull		
Area Final (2)	Notts County (h)	3-0
Bull 2, Downing		
Final	Burnley (Wembley)	2-0
Mutch, Dennison		

Wolves 1988 Sherpa Van Trophy Final team: Kendall, Bellamy, Thompson, Streete, Robertson (Gallagher), Robinson, Dennison, Downing (Vaughan), Bull, Mutch, Holmes.

STEVE BULL IN PARTY MOOD AFTER THE 1988 SHERPA VAN TROPHY VICTORY OVER BURNLEY

THE SECOND STRING

Wolves reserves joined the Central League in 1921 and won the title for the first time in the 1931/32 season. But, like the first team, the 1950s was to bring the second string their finest hours. Five times in the decade they finished as winners of the Central League Championship – in 1951, 52, 53, 58 and 1959. The reserves haven't, however, tasted glory since then. The highest scorer in reserve games for Wolves is Barry Stobart, with 110 in the League and one cup goal whilst Bill Baxter has made the most appearances. The right-half turned out 224 times in reserve League and cup fixtures between 1945 and 1954.

FIVE FINAL VENUES

Wolves and West Bromwich have each contested the FA Cup Final at five different venues – more than any other club. In 1889 Wanderers met Preston at The Oval, in 1893 it was Everton at Fallowfield, three years later came the defeat against Sheffield Wednesday at Crystal Palace – also the venue 12 years on when Newcastle United were in opposition. In 1921, Stamford Bridge housed the final against Tottenham Hotspur whilst the last three finals for Wolves took place in the more familiar surroundings of Wembley Stadium.

UP ANOTHER FLIGHT

After escaping from the Fourth Division at the second attempt in 1988, Wolves won a second successive championship by claiming the Third Division title the following year. Things didn't begin too brightly with a 3-1 reversal against Bury at Gigg Lane. But that was to be one of just three defeats suffered between that opening day and the following March. Steve Bull and Andy Mutch plundered opposition defences and among the victories were heavy beatings of Swansea by 5-2 at the Vetch Field and, at Molineux, Preston (6-0), Mansfield (6-2) and Fulham (5-2). Wanderers' promotion was assured when they beat Bristol City thanks to a Steve Bull brace with four matches remaining – and they were confirmed as Champions two games later after taking a point from a draw with Sheffield United. Andy Thompson was the only ever-present; he played in all 56 League and cup fixtures whilst Bull and Mutch both missed just one game, the final one of the campaign at Wigan when they were both on duty with the England B squad. Bull finished with 37 League goals — just one short of Dennis Westcott's record — and he also scored 13 in cup competitions to take him to the magical half-century mark for the second year in succession. His strike partner Mutch weighed in with 23 as Wolves amassed a total of 116 from 56 League and Cup fixtures.

FOOTBALL LEAGUE DIVISION THREE

		Pl	W	D	L	F	A	W	D	L	F	A	Pts
1	WOLVES	46	18	4	1	61	19	8	10	5	35	30	92
2	Sheffield United	46	16	3	4	57	21	9	6	8	36	33	84
3	Port Vale	46	15	3	5	46	21	9	9	5	32	27	84
4	Fulham	46	12	7	4	42	28	10	2	11	27	39	75
5	Bristol Rovers	46	9	11	3	34	21	10	6	7	33	30	74
6	Preston North End	46	14	7	2	56	31	5	8	10	23	29	72
7	Brentford	46	14	5	4	36	21	4	9	10	30	40	68
8	Chester City	46	12	6	5	38	18	7	5	11	26	43	68
9	Notts County	46	11	7	5	37	22	7	6	10	27	32	67
10	Bolton Wanderers	46	12	8	3	42	23	4	8	11	16	31	64
11	Bristol City	46	10	3	10	32	25	8	6	9	21	30	63
12	Swansea City	46	11	8	4	33	22	4	8	11	18	31	61
13	Bury	46	11	7	5	27	22	5	6	12	28	45	61
14	Huddersfield Town	46	10	8	5	35	25	7	1	15	28	48	60
15	Mansfield Town	46	10	8	5	32	22	4	9	10	16	30	59
16	Cardiff City	46	10	9	4	30	16	4	6	13	14	40	57
17	Wigan Athletic	46	9	5	9	28	22	5	9	9	27	31	56
18	Reading	46	10	6	7	37	29	5	5	13	31	43	56
19	Blackpool	46	10	6	7	36	29	4	7	12	20	30	55
20	Northampton	46	11	2	10	41	34	5	4	14	25	42	54
21	Southend United	46	10	9	4	33	26	3	6	14	23	49	54
22	Chesterfield	46	9	5	9	35	35	5	2	16	16	51	49
23	Gillingham	46	7	3	13	25	32	5	1	17	22	49	40
24	Aldershot	46	7	6	10	29	29	1	7	15	19	49	37

NEUTRAL TERRITORY

Wolves have played just four cup second replays on neutral territory. The first was in February 1904 when Derby County won a second round tie by 1-0 at Villa Park after a pair of two-all draws. In a quarter-final against Sunderland in March 1937, the teams drew 1-1 at Molineux and 2-2 at Roker Park before the Black Cats strolled to a 4-0 victory in the third game at Hillsborough. At a snowy Hawthorns in March 1965, a Hughie McIlmoyle hat-trick put paid to Aston Villa in a fifth round meeting after a one-all draw at Villa Park and a scoreless replay at Molineux. In the successful League Cup season of 1979/80, Wolves earned a place in the semi-finals by beating Grimsby Town by 2-0 at Derby County's Baseball Ground after goalless and one-all draws at Blundell Park and Molineux respectively. Kenny Hibbitt and John Richards gave Wolves followers an early present a week before Christmas in 1979.

PLAY-OFF SUCCESS – AT LAST

Wolves finally ended their play-off hoodoo in 2003 after three fruitless attempts – two of them in the First Division. After finishing sixth in the table, the first leg of the semi-final was against Reading when Shaun Newton and Lee Naylor scored late goals to cancel out Nicky Forster's first-half opener and give Wanderers the slenderest of leads to take to the Madejski Stadium. But Dave Jones' men had the bit between their teeth and an 81st-minute goal from Alex Rae gave them a deserved pass through to the final where Sheffield United lay in wait at the Millennium Stadium. Mark Kennedy's sweetly struck opener helped soothe the nerves and when Nathan Blake headed in from close range after Paul Ince had helped on a Kennedy corner, the promised land of the Premier League was within sight. Just on half-time Kenny Miller converted Shaun Newton's low cross to signal wild celebrations at the opposite end of the ground. There were to be no more goals although the second half wasn't without incident with Matt Murray brilliantly turning away Michael Brown's penalty and then deflecting a Michael Tonge free-kick against the post. Murray's efforts won him the 'Man of the Match' award and, after 14 years of trying (albeit only for a season), Wolves were back in the top flight.

FOOTBALLER OF THE YEAR

Two Wolves players have been named as Footballer of the Year. In 1952, the fifth year of the award, Billy Wright took the honours and then, in 1960, it was Bill Slater that took the coveted title. Whilst he didn't win the European Footballer of the Year title, Billy Wright was amongst the 'candidates' in 1956, 57 and 58 – finishing runner-up behind Real Madrid's Alfredo Di Stefano in the middle of those three years.

HANDY HAMMERS FOR ANDY

Andy Gray, who scored the only goal of the game to give Wolves victory over Nottingham Forest in the 1980 League Cup final, was within two minutes of missing the game altogether. The striker had a one game suspension hanging over his head which he was scheduled to serve a week before the final against Aston Villa in a League fixture. But the Birmingham club had progressed to the FA Cup quarter-finals where they were paired with Second Division West Ham United at Upton Park. The Villa v Wolves game was put back to the following Monday evening but, if the cup-tie finished as a draw, then the replay would have taken precedence over the League fixture and Gray would have had to serve his suspension on the day of the cup final. And it looked as if that was going to be the case until the 88th minute in the East End when Ken McNaught was adjudged to have handled in the penalty area. Ray Stewart smashed home the spot kick to send Gray's former club out of the cup and assure the Scot of a place at Wembley.

FIVE-A-SIDE SUCCESS

Twice in the mid-70s Wolves won the prestigious *Daily Express* Five-A-Side tournament which was staged at the Empire Pool, Wembley. In 1975, the route to the final began with a tied game with Ipswich Town – Alan Sunderland the scorer in a 1-1 draw. Wolves won the resulting penalty shoot-out by 2-1 before an identical score against Stoke City, with Sunderland again on target, leading to another shoot-out and another 2-1 penalty success. Sunderland made it three in three when Wolves overcame Orient by 2-1 in the semi-final with Mike Bailey the other scorer for the Molineux side. The final hurdle was provided by Tottenham Hotspur when goals from Kenny Hibbitt, Bailey and Willie Carr saw Wanderers through to a 3-1 victory. The six-man squad consisted of Gary Pierce, John McAlle, Hibbitt, Bailey, Carr and Sunderland. A year later, Wolves retained the trophy after a controversial final against Stoke. The early rounds had seen a 3-0 triumph over Bristol City – Sunderland with two and Carr the men finding the net. Then, for the second successive year, came a penalty shoot-out win over Ipswich – Wolves winning 3-2 after a goalless eight minutes' play. Steve Daley's left-foot drive saw off the challenge of Glasgow Rangers in the semi-final, and Daley was on target again in the final but Stoke levelled and the game was approaching its conclusion with Wolves well on top when Hibbitt struck a goal that sparked vehement protests from the north Staffordshire side. The midfielder found the net with an indirect free-kick but the referee felt that the ball had clipped the foot of Garth Crooks as it went past Peter Shilton and he awarded the goal. Crooks and his team-mates argued that it wasn't the case and that the ball had gone straight in. Even Hibbitt felt some sympathy by saying that he felt the ball hadn't touched Crooks. But, despite the arguments, as the *Express* reported the next day, Wolves richly deserved their success. Pierce, Carr, Hibbitt and Sunderland again featured in the squad and they were joined by Martin Patching and Daley.

OFF AT THE DOUBLE

When Wolves visited Carrow Road in January 2007, a goal from Michael Kightly was enough to give them three points; not a bad effort considering that they finished the game with just nine men after Gary Breen and Jackie McNamara had both been shown the red card. The next time the teams met, the following September, Wolves again emerged triumphant – 2-0 with goals from Kevin Foley and Andy Keogh. This time it was the Canaries who finished with nine after Jason Shackell and Julian Brellier took early baths after being dismissed.

UP IN STYLE

Wolves ended the 2008/9 campaign at the top of the Championship. Mick McCarthy's men won the title in style, moving into second place after a 2-0 win at Ipswich on August 23 and remaining in the top two for the rest of the season. Going into the New Year, Wanderers held a seven point advantage over second placed Reading, but after picking up just one win and three draws in a nine-game spell in January and February, the gap between first and second narrowed to just three points. But the team found its form at the right time winning eight and drawing two of the eleven games that remained to clinch the championship and finish seven points clear of second place.

FOOTBALL LEAGUE CHAMPIONSHIP

		Pl	W	D	L	F	A	W	D	L	F	A	Gd	Pts
1	WOLVES	46	15	5	3	44	21	12	4	7	36	31	28	90
2	Birmingham C	46	14	5	4	30	17	9	9	5	24	20	17	83
3	Sheffield United	46	12	6	5	35	22	10	8	5	29	17	25	80
4	Reading	46	12	5	6	40	17	9	9	5	32	23	32	77
5	Burnley	46	14	5	4	42	23	7	8	8	30	37	12	76
6	Preston NE	46	16	3	4	39	20	5	8	10	27	34	12	74
7	Cardiff City	46	14	5	4	40	23	5	12	6	25	30	12	74
8	Swansea	46	11	9	3	40	22	5	11	7	23	28	13	68
9	Ipswich Town	46	8	9	6	30	26	9	6	8	32	27	9	66
10	Bristol City	46	7	13	3	30	23	8	3	12	24	31	0	61
11	QPR	46	12	7	4	28	19	3	9	11	14	25	-2	61
12	Sheffield W	46	11	6	6	26	14	5	7	11	25	44	-7	61
13	Watford	46	11	6	6	42	32	5	4	14	26	40	-4	58
14	Doncaster	46	9	5	9	16	18	8	2	13	26	35	-11	58
15	Crystal Palace	46	9	8	6	26	19	6	4	13	26	36	-3	57
16	Blackpool	46	5	8	10	25	33	8	9	6	22	25	-11	56
17	Coventry City	46	8	8	7	26	26	5	7	11	21	32	-11	54
18	Derby County	46	9	7	7	31	26	5	5	13	24	41	-12	54
19	Nottingham F	46	8	7	8	27	28	5	7	11	23	37	-15	53
20	Barnsley	46	8	7	8	28	24	5	6	12	17	34	-13	52
21	Plymouth A	46	7	5	11	31	35	6	7	10	13	22	-13	51
22	Norwich City	46	9	5	9	35	28	3	5	15	22	42	-13	46
23	Southampton	46	4	10	9	23	29	6	5	12	23	40	-23	45
24	Charlton Ath	46	6	8	9	33	38	2	7	14	19	36	-22	39

WOLVES CELEBRATE PROMOTION TO THE PREMIERSHIP IN 2009

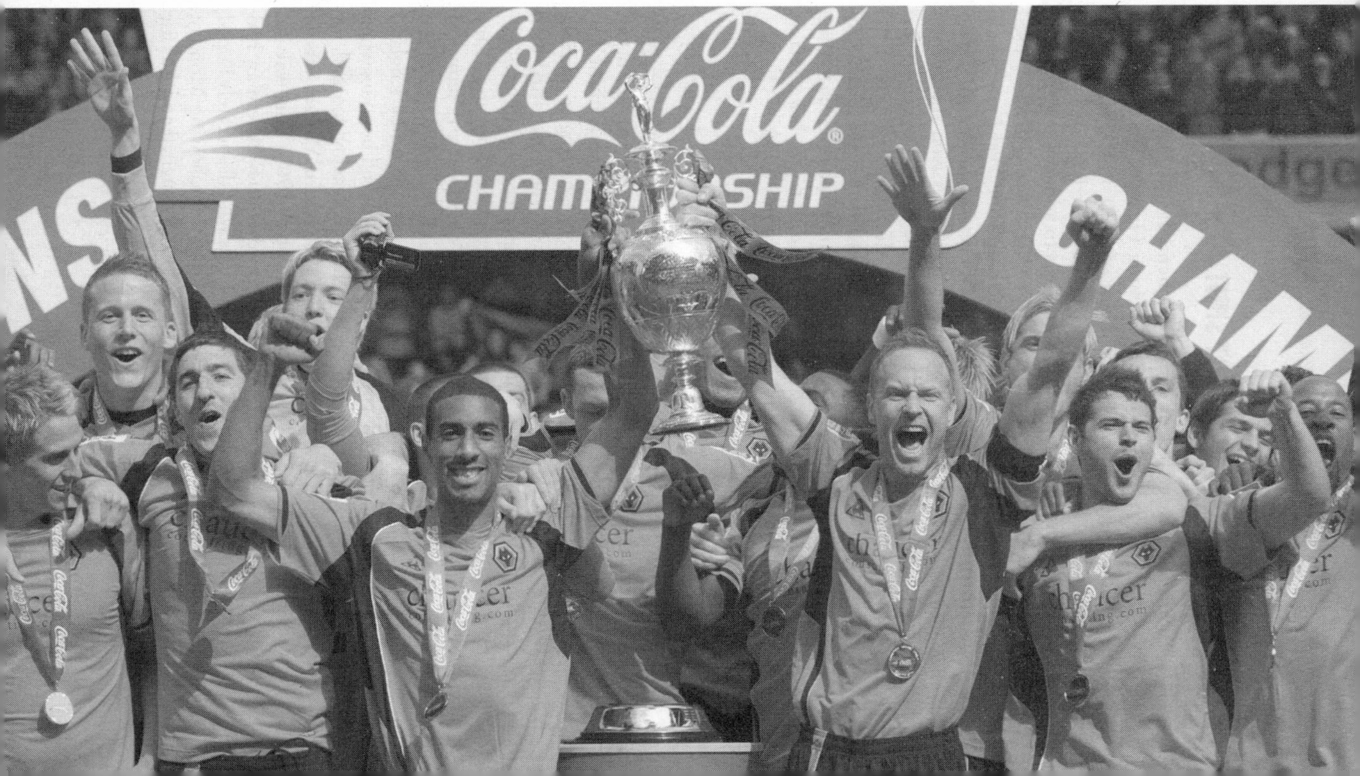

HOT SHOT

Tudor Martin's goal scoring achievements in his short stay with Wolves were, to say the least, eye-catching. He enlisted at Molineux from Newport County in the summer of 1930. In the season that followed he made 12 appearances including the last nine games of the campaign when he scored seven goals to add to the one he had netted a few weeks earlier. But manager Major Frank Buckley used him sparingly in the ensuing campaign and the Welshman made just three further outings and scored once to take his first team tally to nine goals from 15 appearances. Wolves won the Second Division title that season and scored 115 goals in the process so few could argue with the Major's selections. Martin spent much of the term playing for the reserves where he rattled in an incredible 49 goals in League and Cup competitions helping the reserves to their first Central League title. But his efforts didn't save his career at Molineux – he was sold to Swansea Town in July 1932.

GOD'S FOOTBALLER

Peter Knowles stunned the football world when he quit the game to concentrate on being a Jehovah's Witness. As a player he was an enigmatic and temperamental figure who often found himself in trouble for 'winding up' opponents or for back-chatting to officials. But there was little doubt that he was one of the most gifted men ever to pull on a Wolves shirt. Many supporters arguably believe that Peter Broadbent was the greatest ever Wanderer and many felt that Knowles had a lot of Broadbent's attributes. A native of Yorkshire, Knowles arrived at Molineux in October 1962 from the club's nursery team, Wath Wanderers. He was capped by England at youth and Under-23 levels and was tipped for full honours when he announced, at the age of 24, that he was leaving football for religion. The final game of the 191 he played for Wolves was at home to Nottingham Forest in September 1969. The way he joyously celebrated with Derek Dougan after the Ulsterman had scored gave some light to the legions of fans who desperately hoped he wouldn't go through with his threat. But, the following Monday, his kit at the Castlecroft training ground lay untouched and, but for turning out in a handful of testimonial games, his skills were not seen again on a football pitch. For several years Wolves retained his registration in the hope that he would return – but he never did. In 1991, singer/songwriter Billy Bragg wrote a song about him called 'God's Footballer' the lyrics of which are reproduced below. Billy became aware of Knowles' decision after watching a 'Match of the Day' video of sixties action.

> *God's footballer hears the voices of angels*
> *Above the choir at Molineux*
> *God's footballer stands on the doorstep*
> *And brings the Good News of the Kingdom to come*
> *While the crowd sings 'Rock of Ages'*
> *The goals bring weekly wages*
> *Yet the glory of the sports pages*
> *Is but the worship of false idols and tempts him not*
> *God's footballer turns on a sixpence*
> *And brings the Great crowd to their feet in praise of him*
> *God's footballer quotes from the Gospels*
> *While knocking on doors in Black Country back streets*
> *He scores goals on a Saturday*
> *And saves souls on a Sunday*
> *For the Lord says these are the Last Days*
> *Prepare thyself for the Judgement yet to come*
> *His career will be over soon*
> *And the rituals of a Saturday afternoon*
> *Bid him a reluctant farewell*
> *For he knows beyond the sport lies the spiritual*

BILLY FELLS FOREST

Billy Wright gained world renown as a defender but he once hit a hat-trick in just 21 minutes. He played as a forward for Wolves several times during the war. In February 1946, he hit a quickfire treble against Nottingham Forest at Molineux in a Football League (south) fixture. Ray Chatham got the other goal that afternoon in a 4-0 victory. A week earlier, in another home game, Chatham had netted a hat-trick whilst Wright had got the odd goal as Portsmouth were beaten 4-0.

HELLO AND GOODBYE

George Poyser was an instrumental figure in the transfer of Peter Broadbent to Wolves from Brentford in February 1951. Poyser was the manager of Dover when he discovered the talented Broadbent. And it was Poyser – by then a coach at Molineux – who advised the player on the move to Wolves after he had spent less than a year at Griffin Park. Some 13 years later Poyser was managing Manchester City and, on Christmas Eve 1964, he called one of his players to say that Wolves were interested in signing him. That player was left winger Dave Wagstaffe and, on Boxing Day morning, Poyser drove him to Molineux. Waggy recalls signing at noon, having a pre-match meal at the Molineux Hotel and playing in the derby against Aston Villa that afternoon. As the winger made his debut, another member of the home forward line was making his 497th and final appearance for Wanderers – Peter Broadbent.

SWEDISH SOJOURN

In June, 1946 season, Wolves went on a five game tour of Sweden. The first match was against a Gothenburg team comprising 11 players from the city's three clubs. For Wolves, it wasn't the start they had been hoping for as they went down 3-0. To compound matters, Dickie Dorsett was sent off shortly before the final whistle and the travelling directors announced that the striker would take no further part in matches on the tour. Next in line was northern club, Sundsvall, and there was an altogether happier outcome with Dennis Westcott and Johnny Hancocks both hitting two, and Jessie Pye, Fred Ramscar and Tom Galley one each in a Wolves 7-1 win. This was followed by a two-all draw against Gavel when Westcott added another two to his tally, and a 3-1 defeat against Stockholm with Pye the man on target for Wanderers. The trip wound up with a 3-2 win over Malmo. Westcott grabbed his third brace of the tour to put Wolves two goals to the good but the home side hit back to level in an eight-minute spell after the break. Tom Galley was sent off for retaliation before Ray Chatham hit the winner with nine minutes left. After the game, a coach carrying members of both teams to a banquet was surrounded by an angry crowd as it left the ground and several stones were thrown at it.

WANDERERS: READY TO HIT THE ROAD

CRUEL INJURY BLOW

Roy Swinbourne was the two-goal hero on the night that the mighty Honved were beaten at Molineux in the unforgettable 1954 floodlit friendly. Without doubt he was one of the club's greatest forwards and, but for a cruel injury that forced his retirement at the age of just 26, he could have gone on to post a total that would have taken some beating – even by the great Steve Bull. But disaster struck on Guy Fawkes night in 1955 as he was playing his 13th game of the campaign, at Luton Town. In a Wolves attack his momentum took him towards some photographers lined up beside the goal and although he managed to hurdle them, he tore a thigh muscle and didn't play again for four weeks. His return was at Preston and, in a challenge with Deepdale defender Tommy Docherty, Roy's studs got caught in the turf and with the leg already weakened by his earlier injury, further damage was inflicted when knee ligaments were torn. Although he made comeback attempts in reserve games after an operation, the knee kept giving way and sadly he was forced to call it a day. Roy had moved to Molineux as a 15-year-old from Wath Wanderers in 1944 and he signed as a professional two years later. His impressive scoring record was one of a goal in every two games and, in his final season, he had already notched 17 goals and was tipped for full England honours when the injury nightmare began in that unlucky 13th game.

A FUNNY THING HAPPENED ON THE WAY

Aston Villa provided the opposition for a friendly match in September, 1889, to mark the opening of Molineux following the move from Dudley Road. But the Birmingham club didn't have the best of preparations for the game. The team journeyed to Wolverhampton in a carriage pulled by four horses and, whilst travelling through West Bromwich, an axle broke on the vehicle throwing the driver into the road. The players were shaken but unhurt and were able to continue their journey to Wolverhampton on replacement transport. The game itself was decided by a David Wykes goal – the winger connecting with Harry Wood's cross and beating Villa keeper Jack Warner with a low shot. The first League game, five days later, was against Notts County and a crowd of 4,000 saw Wykes on target once more along with Arthur Worrall in a 2-0 victory.

SEMI-FINALS

Wolves have played in 19 FA Cup semi-final games – including five replays – at 14 different venues.

1888/89 v Blackburn Rovers ...... drew 1-1 ....Gresty Road
1888/89 v Blackburn Rovers ...... won 3-1 ....Gresty Road
1889/90 v Blackburn Rovers ...... lost 1-0 ....The Racecourse Ground
1892/93 v Blackburn Rovers ...... won 2-1 ....The Town Ground, Notts
1895/96 v Derby County .... won 2-1 ...... Perry Barr, Birmingham
1907/08 v Southampton .... won 2-0 .... Stamford Bridge
1920/21 v Cardiff City .... drew 0-0 .... Anfield
1920/21 v Cardiff City .... won 3-1 .... Old Trafford
1938/39 v Grimsby Town .... won 5-0 .... Old Trafford
1948/49 v Manchester United ... drew 1-1 ....Hillsborough
1948/49 v Manchester United ... won 1-0 ....Goodison Park
1950/51 v Newcastle United ...... drew 0-0 ....Hillsborough
1950/51 v Newcastle United ...... lost 2-1 ... Leeds Road, Huddersfield
1959/60 v Aston Villa .... won 1-0 .... The Hawthorns
1972/73 v Leeds United............. lost 1-0 ....Maine Road
1978/79 v Arsenal .... lost 2-0 .... Villa Park
1980/81 v Tottenham Hotspur .. drew 2-2 ....Hillsborough
1980/81 v Tottenham Hotspur .. lost 3-0 .... Highbury
1997/98 v Arsenal .... lost 1-0 .... Villa Park

The overall semi-final record for Wolves is won eight, drawn five, lost six with 24 goals scored and 18 conceded.

WANDERERS AVENUE

After Wolves left their Dudley Road ground and moved to Molineux, a local builder and Wolves supporter constructed houses on the site. On the walls of houses in Wanderers Avenue he inscribed the names of some of the club's early stars including members of the triumphant 1893 FA Cup winning side. In Dudley Road, a plaque commemorating the Cup win, bearing a carving of the trophy, was placed above the doors of numbers 329 and 330. Sadly, the houses were demolished to make way for a garage in the seventies although Wanderers Avenue still exists.

WHAT A START

John Richards scored what is believed to be the fastest goal in the history of the club in a competitive fixture. Playing against Burnley at Turf Moor in November 1975, Richards converted a low cross from John Farley from close quarters after just 15 seconds.

HUGE CUP TURNOUTS

A grand total of 168,507 spectators watched Wolves and Sunderland battling it out for a place in the 1937 FA Cup semi-final. It took three games before the Black Cats finally made it through to meet Millwall in the last four with 57,751 watching the one-all draw at Molineux and 61,796 the replay at Roker Park when the sides shared four goals. The decider was played at Hillsborough with 48,960 viewing a 4-0 Sunderland victory. The Wearside team beat Millwall and then, in the final at Wembley, overcame Preston North End by 3-1.

ALL AT ONCE

Liverpool-born John McAlle is sixth in the all-time appearances record list for Wolves with 508 outings between 1968 and 1981. The central defender only scored three goals for the club and they all came in a three-week spell in September 1971. He opened his account in the 4-3 League Cup defeat at Manchester City and was then on target in the home and away wins over Academica Coimbra in a first round UEFA Cup tie.

LIGHTING UP TIME

In 1953 Wolves provided the opposition in friendly games to mark the opening of floodlights at Bristol City, Hull City, Bilston Town (or Bilston Borough as they were then known), Bury and Hednesford Town – where they took on and beat arch rivals West Bromwich Albion 4-2. The moment Molineux fans were waiting for arrived in September 1953 when Wolves met South Africa in the first floodlit game at the ground.